Memoirs from
Mrs. Hudson's Kitchen

Columns from *Canadian Holmes*

by Wendy Heyman-Marsaw

Edited and compiled

by JoAnn and Mark Alberstat

Paperback ISBN 978-1-78705-180-5
ePub ISBN 978-1-78705-181-2
PDF ISBN 978-1-78705-182-9

Published in the UK by MX Publishing
335 Princess Park Manor, Royal Drive,
London, N11 3GX
www.mxpublishing.co.uk

Cover design by Brian Belanger

Dedication

To my first "S.H." – Sidney Heyman – who introduced me to the world of Sherlock Holmes. He was also the only man I ever saw wear a deerstalker on the New York City subway.

And to my husband, Dean, for his love, encouragement and support for "Mrs. Hudson" from day one.

A special thanks to my Sherlockian cheering section: Jonathan and Christina, Stephanie and Tyson, Lynn, Nemo and Nico.

With much appreciation to Mark and JoAnn Alberstat, without whom this book would not have been possible.

Contents

Preface

It all began in New York City with my youthful indoctrination into the Sherlockian world at the age of 8 when I was given my first copy of the *Adventures of Sherlock Holmes* by my father, Sidney Heyman. He was an unabashed pipe-smoking Anglophile and Sherlockian devotee who regularly sported a deerstalker. Family outings included visits to Gillette Castle and to see Fritz Weaver on Broadway in the 1965 musical *Baker Street*.

I was offered an opportunity to attend university in London for a year in 1972.My first impression of London was that I was living in an atmospheric movie set quite like the Basil Rathbone films I had avidly watched. Thus inspired, I joined The Sherlock Holmes Society of London and visited as many of the locales that were detailed in the Canon as possible.

I then had the pleasure of working with Chris Steinbrunner, a member of The Baker Street Irregulars. Among other accomplishments he won an Edgar Award for *The Encyclopedia of Mystery and Detection*. We would have long talks about his BSI meetings, various Sherlockian books and topics. I always gained fresh insights into the Canon after our discussions.

My attachment to the Sherlockian lore never waned over the next 30 years as an ex-pat living and working in advertising in Canada. During this period I was captivated by the acclaimed Granada Jeremy Brent productions of the Sherlock Holmes stories. Here was a Holmes and Watson that for me truly represented the characters depicted in the novels and short stories.

Upon my retirement to Halifax from Toronto, I contacted Mark Alberstat and joined the local Spence Munro Sherlockian society. As a member I received a copy of *Canadian Holmes*, the quarterly journal of the Bootmakers of Toronto. Mark had a small column titled "Mrs. Hudson's Kitchen," which provided a recipe from the Victorian era. The column inspired me to approach Mark and his wife JoAnn, editors of the journal, with a proposal to expand the scope of the article to elaborate on the role of Mrs. Hudson in the Canon, links to various Victorian social influences and recipes pertaining to the subject of each column.

I had always been dissatisfied with media depictions of Mrs. Hudson as an aged and fussy member of the 221B household. It seemed to me that Mrs. Hudson had a completely privileged, unique perspective on and intimate knowledge of the lives of her illustrious tenants. She is a quiet yet compelling presence in the life of the two men who treated her with the grace and dignity she accorded to them. Additionally, she could build a bridge from the Canon to the various influences of the Victorian mores and their impact on the society in which Holmes and Watson flourished. My image of Mrs. Hudson evolved to be a more contemporary figure to Holmes and Watson. After all, she had to be flexible, understanding, involved and sympathetic to the rather eccentric and extraordinary lives of her tenants. Her loyalty and discretion are exemplary. True, Conan Doyle does not provide much direct evidence about her character, but the implication is there – from literally crawling on her hands and knees to assist Holmes in the "The Adventure of the Empty House" to her tolerance for unpredictable behaviours on the part of Mr. Holmes in particular. Interest in their work and well-being seemed to be uppermost in her mind. Indeed, her hysteria in "The Dying Detective" demonstrates just how much she cared for Holmes and respected Dr. Watson.

The columns also permitted me to indulge my thirst for knowledge of the Victorian era through research on many topics related to Mrs. Hudson. Additionally, the columns enabled me to immerse myself deeper into the Canon in general.

Three books provided much-needed information and indispensable inspiration for the columns: Jack Tracy's *Encyclopedia Sherlockiana, Mrs. Beeton's Book of Household Management* and *A History of Everyday Things in England Volume IV 1851-1914* by Marjorie and C.H.B. Quennell. Another often used reference was Leslie S. Klinger's *The New Annotated Sherlock Holmes*. My collection of British cookbooks, several of which offered regional and historical information, were valuable sources for the recipes. My home library also has a robust representation on Victoriana in general. The internet provided much-needed historical factual evidence and data regarding the Victorian era.

I am still member of the Sherlock Holmes Society of London as well as The Bootmakers of Toronto, which awarded me the honour of Master Bootmaker (MBt) in 2016 as a result of my work on the columns. The Spence Munros of Halifax provided encouraging fellowship and good humour about the articles. I would like to thank these organizations for their support for the columns. Roger Johnson of the London Society kindly provided the source of several quotes from the Canon, as did Mark Alberstat.

I am indebted to JoAnn and Mark Alberstat for their editing and willingness to include Mrs. Hudson's expanded memoirs in *Canadian Holmes*. Their continued support and encouragement led to the publication of this book. Without their efforts and guidance, it would never have been possible.

6

Finally, I would like to thank my husband, Dean, for his wise and meaningful contributions – including the title of this book. My Sherlockian family never waned in expressing their delight over every column. My son Jonathan and his wife Christina accompanied me to the Silver Blaze Race event in Toronto. Jon also took me to the Sherlock special exhibit at the Canadian National Exhibition. My daughter Stephanie and her partner Tyson were involved with the design and execution of my "Sherlock Lives!" tattoo. And my sister Lynn, her husband Nemo and my niece Nico were my Californian Sherlockian cheerleaders from the very start.

In all, the work on the Mrs. Hudson columns was truly enlightening and a joy for me to write. And I hope it makes Mrs. Hudson's character and her times more multi-dimensional for the reader as well. Enjoy the recipes!

Wendy Heyman-Marsaw, MBt.
Halifax, Nova Scotia
June 2017

Introduction

The first issue of *Canadian Holmes* appeared in the fall of 1973 as a newsletter. Six years later it had become a quarterly digest-sized journal and it has remained that way since. Today, there is an international readership and the authors featured inside span the globe. Readers not only enjoy well-researched and written articles, there are also toasts, songs, poems and illustrations. We try to make the journal something for everyone. The journal is available by subscription and all journals since 2009 are also available online.

We took over the editorship of the journal in 2009 and began to put our own stamp on the content. Early on, Wendy Heyman-Marsaw offered her writing skills to a Mrs. Hudson column that we happily took on. The column quickly became a popular feature in each issue. Years later Mark realized that the body of work was significant enough to form a book, approached MX Publishing and the result is in your hand. The original journal columns have changed order, and gained recipes and illustrations. This is not exactly the Mrs. Hudson columns that appeared in *Canadian Holmes*.

We hope you enjoy this eclectic mix of Victorian history, commentary and recipes.

Mark and JoAnn Alberstat
Dartmouth, Nova Scotia
June 2017

Breakfast – Starting the day

"Her cuisine is a little limited, but she has as good an idea of breakfast as a Scotchwoman."

— Sherlock Holmes in "The Naval Treaty"

The English breakfast owes much to the Scots. They eat more substantial breakfasts than the English, Welsh or Irish. Scottish influence is evident every time one eats porridge, kippers, sausage or marmalade, which was first produced in the 1790s by Keiller of Dundee. I always provide a hearty meal for Mr. Holmes and Dr. Watson, for it may be the only sustenance they have for a protracted period of time.

My two gentlemen enjoy upper-class Victorian breakfasts when working for well-to-do clients. Such meals include, at minimum, fruit and porridge; cold tomatoes and ham; fancy rolls; assorted jams and marmalades; bacon; sausages and mushrooms; boiled, fried and scrambled eggs; toast; kedgeree; kidneys and broiled kippers, plus tea and coffee. The middle classes enjoy a more traditional English breakfast consisting of bacon, sausage, fried eggs, fried bread, fried potatoes and grilled tomatoes. Colonel Arthur R. Kenney-Herbert wrote a very good cookery book, *Fifty Breakfasts*, in 1894 for middle-class families of six. This book, I am told, is still available today for those who want to order it and enjoy a Victorian breakfast. Kenney-Herbert, who wrote under the pseudonym of Wyvern, also wrote about Indian cookery. I wonder if Dr. Watson ever met him?

Recipes

Kedgeree– Serves 4
Ingredients: ½ cup of rice, 4 large hard boiled eggs, 1lb cooked whitefish (haddock, turbot, sole, salmon or pike) or ½ white and ½ smoked haddock or salmon for a stronger flavour, 1Tbsp. butter, salt, pepper.

Mode: Cook rice until tender. Chop hard boiled eggs into small pieces. Flake fish finely and mix all together with rice and eggs. Put the mixture into a large saucepan with 1Tbsp. of butter. Cook it until thoroughly hot, stirring constantly to prevent burning. Season with salt and pepper and serve very hot. Take care not to make it too moist.

Savoury Eggs– Serves 1-2
Ingredients: 1-2 oz. cooked bacon, chopped parsley, pepper, 2 large eggs, salt, 1 Tbsp. whole milk or cream.

Mode: Dice bacon, mix with parsley and season with pepper. For each serving, put in a small tart tin or serving dish. Beat 2 eggs with a little salt, 1 Tbsp. of milk or cream, and pour over bacon. Bake in a moderate oven until the eggs are set.

Mushrooms on Toast – Serves 2
Ingredients: 9 oz. white button mushrooms, 1 tsp. oil, 1 Tbsp. butter plus extra for spreading, 4 Tbsp. heavy cream, freshly grated nutmeg, 2 thick slices of bread, chopped chives or parsley for garnish, salt and ground fresh pepper

Mode: Clean and trim mushrooms and cut into thick slices. Heat the oil and butter in a non-stick pan, add the sliced mushrooms and cook quickly for about 3 minutes, stirring frequently. Stir in cream and season with salt, pepper and a little nutmeg. Simmer 1-2 minutes. Toast the bread and spread with butter. Top with the mushrooms, sprinkle with the chopped herbs and serve.

Crumpets – Makes 10 - 12
Ingredients: 2 cups all-purpose flour, ½ tsp. salt, ½ tsp. baking soda, 1 tsp. fast-acting yeast granules, 2/3 cup of whole milk, oil for greasing, scant 1 cup water (about 7 oz.)

Mode: Sift the flour, salt, baking soda into a bowl and stir in the yeast. Make a well in the centre. Heat the milk with scant cup of water until lukewarm and pour into the well. Mix well with whisk or wooden spoon, beating vigorously to make a thick, smooth batter. Cover and leave in a warm space for about 1 hour until the mixture has a spongy texture. Heat a griddle or heavy frying pan. Lightly oil the hot surface and the inside of 3 or 4 metal rings, each measuring 3 ½ inches in diameter. Place the oiled rings on the hot surface and leave 1-2 minutes until hot. Spoon the batter into the rings to a depth of about ½ inch. Cook over medium-high heat for about 6 minutes until the top surface is set and bubbles have burst open to make holes. When set, carefully lift off the metal rings and flip the crumpets over, cooking the second side for just 1 minute until lightly browned. Lift off and cool completely on wire rack. Repeat with the remaining crumpet mixture. Just before serving, toast the crumpets on both sides and butter generously.

SWEET REFLECTIONS

"No Better Food." —DR. ANDREW WILSON, F.R.S.E., &c.

Fry's Pure Concentrated **Cocoa**

300 Gold Medals, &c.

"The Most Perfect Form of Cocoa. —Guy's Hospital Gazette.

The Irregulars come to call

"What on earth is this? I cried, for at this moment, there came the pattering of many steps in the hall, and on the stairs, accompanied by audible expressions of disgust upon the part of our landlady. It's the Baker Street division of the detective force, said my companion gravely; and as he spoke there rushed into the room half a dozen of the dirtiest and most ragged street Arabs that I ever clapped eyes on. "

– Dr. John H. Watson in *A Study in Scarlet*

You must remember that Mr. Holmes had but recently occupied rooms at 221B. I didn't know what to think his intentions were. The urchins' loud and disorderly conduct, filthy bodies and clothes were extremely distressing. I feared for my lovely rugs and pristine walls. Then I heard Mr. Holmes call them to attention and directed Wiggins – the eldest, and I suppose the leader of this band of mud larks – to represent the group in future. Mr.

"IT'S THE BAKER STREET DIVISION OF THE DETECTIVE POLICE FORCE'"

Holmes further explained their usefulness in gaining information for his cases.

I had little exposure to children, as my dear husband passed away before we could start a family. I began to reconsider my first impressions and reflected on the difficult lives of the children. Some may have been orphans or cast aside by parents who could not afford to keep them. Many wore unmatched boots and ill-fitting ragged clothing. Baths and regular meals were alien to them. I discovered one to be a little girl who never had a dress or doll.

Mr. Holmes was no doubt the first person of the upper classes to value them, accord them dignity and offer money to improve their lot for work well done. He paid them a shilling a day with a guinea bonus for the one who found the object of their investigation. I was shamed by my initial uncharitable and superficial response. From that day forward I invited the children into my kitchen and fed them simple, nourishing meals and a treat for their pudding. All I asked was that they wash their hands and faces in the scullery sink.

Recipes

Toad-In-The-Hole– Serves 6
Ingredients: 6 oz. flour, 2 cups whole milk, 3 eggs, butter, slices of leftover mutton, 2 fine cleaned and diced kidneys (or substitute 6 good-quality beef or pork sausages), pepper and salt.

Mode: Make a smooth batter of flour, milk, eggs in the above proportion; butter a baking dish, and pour in the batter. Into this place slices of mutton, kidneys or the sausages; bake about 1 hour or rather longer if needed, and send it to the table in the dish it was baked in.

Bread and Butter Pudding – serves 6-8

Ingredients: 8 Tbsp. butter, softened, 12 thin slices homemade-type white bread, ½ cup dried currants, ½ cup sultana raisins, 1/8 tsp. ground cinnamon, 5 large eggs, 3 cups whole milk, 1 cup heavy cream, ¼ cup sugar, pinch of nutmeg. Garnish with whipped cream or ice cream.

Mode: With a pastry brush, coat bottom and sides of a 7x 10 x 2 ½ - inch baking dish with 2 Tbsp. of the butter. Trim and discard crusts of the bread, and butter it liberally on both sides. Place 4 slices of the bread side by side on the bottom of the dish, and trim them to fit snugly. Toss the currants, raisins and cinnamon together in a small bowl, and strew half of the mixture over the bread. Add a second layer of bread, strew the remainder of the fruit over it, and top with a final layer of bread. With a whisk or rotary beater, beat the eggs to a froth in a large mixing bowl. Beat in the milk, cream, sugar and nutmeg, and then pour the mixture evenly over the bread. Let the pudding rest at room temperature for at least 30 minutes, or until the bread has absorbed almost all of the liquid. Preheat oven to 350F. Cover the pudding with a lightly buttered sheet of foil and bake in the middle of the oven for 30 minutes. Remove foil and bake for 30 minutes longer or until the top is crisp and golden brown. Serve hot, directly from the baking dish. Garnish with whipped cream or ice cream if desired.

Bubble and squeak

Ingredients: 3 cups chopped, cold cooked potatoes crushed slightly, ¼ cup drippings or lard (do not substitute), 1 medium onion, minced, 1 ½ cups chopped cooked cabbage or Brussels sprouts, salt and freshly ground pepper.

15

Mode: In a heavy frying pan, melt half the fat and lightly fry the onion. Mix in the potato and greens, and season well with salt and pepper. Add more drippings or lard. Press the bubble into the hot fat and fry over moderate heat until browned underneath – about 15 minutes. Turn the bubble over, add the last of the drippings or lard, and fry until the other side is browned.

Kitchen Innovation – The path forward

"It was the era … of the scientist and civil engineer as hero. Holmes's profession as a consulting detective depended on just the right combination of cultural elements – popular acceptance of scientific principles…."

– Jack Tracy in *The Encyclopedia Sherlockiana*

Ever since the Great Crystal Palace Exhibition of 1851, spearheaded by Prince Albert, Consort of Queen Victoria, advances in modern technology and design increased consistently in Britain, as well as other developed countries. "World's Fairs" originally began in 1756 and continue to the present day. It has been said that the 19th century gave birth to the professional scientist. The word "scientist" was first used in 1833.

I was fascinated by the flurry of new inventions, particularly those of practical use in the home. It was fortunate that Mr. Holmes and Dr. Watson were early adopters of new technology as it related to their work. They encouraged me to seek new items for our household. I selected items that were most practical. My first acquisition was a telephone apparatus. It made common sense given Mr. Holmes's and Dr. Watson's occupations. I also changed our door locks to Mr. Yale's sturdy design. Again, a prudent act since some of our visitors were rather malevolent.

I added large and small items for my own use. The gas cooking range was introduced at the 1883 Paris Exposition. An electric one followed just a few years later. I purchased a gas type. Many cookery books were available for gas ranges, and professional chefs touted their ability to adjust heat more quickly and precisely.

Firms that sold ice began to sell insulated ice chests. They were popular and available in small to very substantial sizes. Other helpful devices included a rotary whisk that reduced the time to beat egg whites by half. Meat mincers, sausage machines, apple and potato parers, cucumber slicers, radish scrapers and pea shellers were popular. Food preserved in tins had many advantages: one could enjoy items out of season, store formerly perishable goods and keep a nicely stocked pantry without a daily visit to the shops. Some attempts were more successful than others but new varieties were introduced frequently.

A rotary knife cleaner and dishwasher were also available, but unnecessary in our little household. By 1886 technology and scientists gave us such valuable items as the lightbulb, Bissell carpet sweeper, fountain pen, sewing machine, typewriter, zippers, bicycle frame, gramophone, coffee percolators and by 1901, the vacuum cleaner. Please forgive this delicate subject, but the invention of paper for personal sanitation was greatly appreciated and improved household hygiene considerably.

Below are some new recipes that utilized the insulated ice chest. It was thoroughly enjoyed by Mr. Holmes and Dr. Watson.

Recipes

Blackcurrant Cream Ice – Serves 4

Ingredients: 1 lb. blackcurrants, 1 cup syrup made with I cup sugar and ½ cup water, ½ cup heavy cream. To decorate: crystallized cherries, candied angelica, preserved fruits.

Mode: Clean blackcurrants, stir and mash them over the fire for 5 minutes then pass them through a fine-hair sieve. Mix the syrup, at 92F, with the blackcurrant puree and cream. When well beaten together, turn the mixture into the freezing part of the ice chest and work until stiff. Put the cream in a fluted metal mould, close it, pack in ice and leave in ice chest until frozen. Dip the mould in lukewarm water, wipe it and turn the cream out on a fancy dish.

Decorate with cherries, angelica cut into points and garnish round with preserved apples, pears or other fruit. Surmount the whole with an ornamental attelette and set in ice chest to keep cold until wanted. This is reckoned to be one of the finest flavoured and handsomest sweets that can be prepared.

No Churn Mint Chip Ice Cream

Ingredients: 14 oz. tin sweetened condensed milk, 2 tsp. peppermint extract, 1 Tbs. crème de menthe, 2 cups chilled heavy whipping cream, pinch of coarse salt, 1 cup chopped bittersweet (70% cacao) chocolate.

Mode: In a large bowl, stir together condensed milk, peppermint extract, and crème de menthe. In another bowl, beat heavy cream with salt until stiff peaks form. Gently fold into milk mixture, in two batches, until no streaks are left. Fold in chocolate. Transfer to a loaf pan; freeze for at least 6 hours and up to 1 month.

Lemon Sorbet – Makes about 5 cups

Garnish with lemon zest, fresh berries or mint. Lovely served in chilled halved hollowed lemon cups.

Ingredients: 1 3/4 cups water, 2 cups sugar, 2 cups freshly squeezed lemon juice 1 to 2 Tbsp. freshly grated lemon zest.

Mode: In a small saucepan over medium heat, combine the water and sugar, and boil until the sugar dissolves, about 1 minute. Remove from heat and allow to cool. Stir in the lemon juice and lemon zest, then pour into a 9 x 13 inch metal baking pan. Freeze until firm (about 2-3 hours), stirring with a fork every ½ hour. Cover tightly or transfer to freezer container. Will keep up to 1 month.

Tea for two

Although my gentlemen prefer coffee at breakfast and dinner, they request a cream tea from time to time when expecting a client or a visit from Mr. Mycroft. At Baker Street we dine at 7 unless Mr. Holmes and Dr. Watson plan an evening's entertainment. They usually dine out after the performance and so will take tea at 4 or 5 o'clock.

Some foreigners confuse a cream tea with "high tea." High tea is the evening dinner for the nursery and the middle classes. It is a single course that includes a variety of dishes such as hot or cold meats and pies, stews and eggs. Cream teas were introduced when dinner in affluent households began to be served at increasingly late hours. A proper cream tea is a three-course service. I own a lovely and helpful three-tiered platter stand that permits me to carry all three courses at once up our 17 steps.

Tea begins with scones, clotted or Devonshire cream and preserves. Dainty, crustless sandwiches such as cucumber and watercress, chicken or egg salad are served in small decorative shapes. These comprise the second, or savoury course, for women. Men prefer more substantial fare such as sliced beef with chutney, ham with mustard and smoked salmon. Gentlemen's Relish, an anchovy paste created by Mr. Osborne in 1828 according to a secret recipe, is served on buttered white-bread toast. The third course is a selection of small sweets such as petit fours, thin slices of Dundee or fruitcake. Battenberg cake has become popular since it was served at the 1884 marriage of Queen Victoria's granddaughter, Princess Victoria, to Prince Louis of Battenberg.

Some people serve only thinly sliced bread and butter. That is rather inhospitable, to my mind.

I purchase our tea at Twinings of London (Est.1706), located nearby on the Strand. Mr. Holmes is partial to Darjeeling, from the foothills of the Himalayas. Dr. Watson acquired a taste for Assam whilst in India. They are both varieties of black teas. Twinings informed me that tea drinking did not begin in England. The Dutch were first to import and partake of tea, followed by the French. It is my opinion, however, that none do it as well as the English.

To brew a perfect pot, you must begin with a kettle of fresh, cold water that has never been boiled. For black tea, you will want the water at a full rolling boil. Remove it from the hob and let it cool a minute or two. Warm the teapot with a bit of the boiling water, swirl and discard. Add one teaspoon of tea per person, and one more for the pot, and pour the boiled water over it. Let it steep for three to five minutes. To serve, pour tea into each cup through a porcelain strainer. Accompany with sugar cubes, honey, milk, cream or lemon.

> "The naming of teas is a difficult matter,
> It isn't just one of your everyday games-
> Some might think you as mad as a hatter
> Should you tell them each goes by several names.
> For starters each tea in this world must belong
> To the families Black or Green or Oolong;
> Then look more closely as these family trees-
> Some include Indians along with Chinese."
> — T.S. Eliot

In service to Mr. Holmes

Mrs. Hudson was a long-suffering woman. Not only was her first floor flat invaded at all hours by throngs of singular and often undesirable characters, but her remarkable lodger showed an eccentricity and irregularity in his life which must have sorely tried her patience. His incredible untidiness, his addiction to music at strange hours, his occasional revolver practice within doors, his weird and often malodorous scientific experiments, and the atmosphere of violence and danger which hung about him made him the very worst tenant in London.

> – Dr. John H. Watson in "The Dying Detective"

Despite dear Dr. Watson's observations, I never had cause to seriously regret being Mr. Holmes's landlady and occasional hostess. Indeed, I take pride in my small role supporting his unique work as a consulting detective. He treated me with the utmost courtesy and respect. Whenever possible, he was mindful to inform me of his chaotic schedule and commitments.

Ours was a small but unpredictably busy household. My variety of duties necessitated assistance. I engaged a cook, Mrs. Violet Turner, my sister-in-law. Flexible hours and duties meant she could earn some pin money without neglecting her family. The maid-of-all-work, Molly, was only 14 but efficient and hard working. We had two pageboys, both named Billy. They ran numerous errands for Mr. Holmes and occasionally assisted me in greeting and directing clients. The pages ran up and down our stairs constantly. They slept in a small alcove to be handy for jobs at all hours. Our second Billy was a favourite of Dr. Watson and Mr. Holmes. When he outgrew his position, he joined Scotland Yard.

My responsibilities were many as landlady and occasionally housekeeper. I paid the bills for all the upkeep of 221 Baker Street. My housekeeping-accounts book was kept daily and precisely. *Mrs. Beeton's Book of Household Management* outlines the qualities of a good housekeeper thusly: "honesty, industry and vigilance...as if she were the head of her own family. Cleanliness, punctuality and method are essentials in character." Method was a trait highly valued by Mr. Holmes.

Additional domestic duties included preparing breakfast for my gentlemen (who, thankfully, slept later than most). In the kitchen, I had superintendence of menus and meals preparation. I baked bread, pastries and cakes, and put up preserves and relishes. I noted when to replenish supplies and ensure the entire kitchen was scrubbed and the stove cleaned and prepared for the next day.

The cleaning of 221B was sometimes amusing and often a frustrating challenge. Molly and I had to work together. I provided the complex direction regarding Mr. Holmes's somewhat odd preferences. The only time their rooms got a thorough cleaning was when they were pursuing a case outside London. Their bedrooms provided insight into their habits. Mr. Holmes's bed was never made and linens and pillows were often left on the floor. His argument was that he will only sleep in it again the next night or not at all. Although a man of impeccable personal cleanliness, his wardrobe was in complete disarray, save his evening wear. His well-worn mouse-coloured dressing gown appeared anywhere in the rooms. The good doctor, however, never forgot his army training. His room was neat as a pin – bed perfectly made, clothes hung in orderly fashion and window open for airing.

The parlour was daunting at times. Mr. Holmes claimed to have complete order in the mountain of disorder. Since Dr. Watson and Mr. Holmes were heavy smokers, it was essential to air the room and wash windows, looking glasses and glassware, etc. Often Molly and I were assaulted by disgusting odours emanating from the chemistry apparatus. Dust and ash lay everywhere. Newspapers, particularly the agony columns, were strewn all over the floor. If we gathered them in a neat pile to clean the rugs, Mr. Holmes would become quite agitated. So I simply lifted the papers whilst Molly cleaned under them. Remnants of aged meals would occasionally be discovered as well.

For now, you may welcome these recipes for useful and effective household aids:

To Restore Whiteness to Scorched Linen
Ingredients: 1 cup vinegar, 2 oz. fuller's earth, 1 oz. of dried fowl's dung

An Excellent Pomatom (Hair Pomade)
Ingredients: ½ lb. lard, 1 cup olive oil, 1 cup castor oil, 4 oz. spermaceti, bergamot or any other scent, elderflower water

To Clean Marble
Mix with ¼ cup of soap lees, 4 oz. of turpentine, sufficient pipe-clay and bullock's gall to make the whole into a rather thick paste. Apply it to the marble with a soft brush, and after a day or two, when quite dry, rub it off with a soft rag. Apply this a second or third time till the marble is quite clean.

Polish for Boots

Take 4 oz. of ivory-black and 4 oz. of treacle, 1 oz. sulphuric acid, 2 spoonfulls of your best olive oil, 3 ½ cups of your best white wine vinegar: mix the ivory-black and treacle well in an earthen jar; then add the sulphuric acid, continuing to stir the mixture; next pour in the oil; and lastly, add the vinegar, stirring it in by degrees, until thoroughly incorporated.

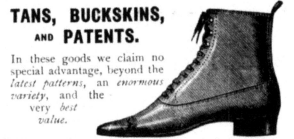

The joint

"He (Holmes) cut a slice of beef from the joint upon the sideboard, sandwiched it between 2 rounds of bread, and thrusting this crude meal into his pocket he started off on his expedition."

— Dr. John H. Watson – "The Beryl Coronet"

A joint of beef is the culinary centrepiece of English cuisine. A joint is, according to *The Cambridge Dictionary*: "(noun) A large piece of meat which is cooked in one piece; a piece of meat for cooking, usually containing a bone. Derivation: Middle English from Old French, from past participle of joindre, to join. A piece of meat roasted or for roasting and of a size for slicing into more than one portion." It is common practice to roast a joint for Sunday dinner and eat the leftovers for the rest of the week, hence the joint on the sideboard referred to above.

The royal guards at The Tower of London are commonly known "Beefeaters," a sobriquet they dislike. Their official title is: Yeoman Warders of her Majesty's Royal Palace and Fortress the Tower of London, and Members of the Sovereign's Body Guard of the Yeoman Guard Extraordinaire. The name Beefeaters may date back to William the Conqueror's construction of the Tower in 1078 and is most likely based upon The Warders' right to eat as much beef as they desired from the king's table.

I have fond memories of my family's cook roasting the joint on a spit that was turned by smoke jacks. This is a device that fit into the chimney and turned when a current of hot air and smoke hit

27

them, in turn rotating another wheel to which a chain was attached. The chain stretched down to a wheel fastened to the spit and so the spit rotated. The hotter the fire, the faster the jack went around.

Mr. Holmes and Dr. Watson savoured the excellent joints served in Simpson's-in-the-Strand. In "The Illustrious Client," Dr. Watson met Mr. Holmes there twice during the course of that case. Dr. Watson wrote, "...I met him by appointment that evening at Simpson's, where sitting at a small table in the front window, and looking down at the rushing stream of life in the Strand, he told me something of what had passed." Of the second visit he wrote: "I did not see Holmes again until the following evening when we dined once more at our Strand restaurant. In "The Dying Detective," Mr. Holmes said, "When we have finished at the police station I think that something nutritious at Simpson's would not be out of place."

Simpson's-in-the-Strand has a curious history. It was opened in 1828 as the Grand Cigar Divan. It developed into a coffee house where gentlemen smoked cigars, drank coffee, browsed the newspapers and played chess – which had a prominent role in Simpson's history. The Grand Cigar Divan became recognized as the 'Home of Chess' in England. Today, one of Simpson's original chess sets is displayed in the front hall. There is always a chess set available for those wishing to play. In 1848 the owner, Mr. Reiss, became partners with caterer John Simpson. They enlarged the premises and renamed it Simpson's and Divan Tavern. The quality of food and drink introduced by Mr. Simpson became a favourite with London's epicures. He also introduced the practice of wheeling large joints of meat on sterling silver dinner wagons to tables and carving the meat in front of the diners — a custom upheld today with the original trolleys still in service. Edmund William Cathie Scott next owned the restaurant. In 1898 Sir

Richard D'Oyly Carte purchased Simpson's. He refurbished and reopened under the name Simpson's-in-the-Strand Grand Divan Tavern, which became known as Simpson's. The current bill of fare lists roast rib of Scottish Beef with roast potatoes, Savoy cabbage, Yorkshire pudding & horseradish for £27.50.

A wall plaque honouring distinguished guests is displayed in the Front Room of Simpson's-in-the-Strand. Among such luminaries as Charles Dickens, Winston Churchill, Benjamin Disraeli and William Gladstone is the name Mr. Sherlock Holmes.

Recipes

Prime Rib Roast– Serves 4
Ingredients: Minimum 5 lbs. prime beef rib roast (Black Angus, if available). Larger roasts are tastier. A three-rib roast is about the smallest desirable size. A 5-rib roast is an elegant dish and for a large party, a seven- or eight-rib roast is a sight to be seen — if your oven is big enough to hold it. The roast should be tied and suet placed on top for self-basting. Let meat stand out of fridge for several hours before roasting. Salt and pepper. Four to six cloves minced garlic or more to taste.

Mode: Rub roast with salt, pepper and garlic. Put roast in an uncovered roasting pan. Use a rack if you have one. The best way to be sure of the state of doneness is to use a meat thermometer. Heat oven to 450F– 500F. Cook meat at this temperature for 25 minutes or until it is well seared. Lower temperature to 325F and continue cooking (without basting). Rare beef 16-18 minutes per pound, med-rare – 20-22 minutes per pound, medium – 24-26 minutes per pound, well-done – 30 minutes per pound If using a thermometer: 120F for rare beef, medium-rare — 130F, medium — 140F, well done – 150F. Let meat stand for 15-30 minutes before carving, as the roast will continue to cook after being removed from the oven, the juices will settle and the texture will be firmer.

MARKETING GUIDE: BEEF.

1. Round. 2. Aitchbone. 3. Brisket. 4. Tongue. 5. Leg. 6. Ribs. 7. Sirloin.
8. Buttock; E. Topside or Buttock; F. Silverside or Round. 9. Hind-quarter:
A. Leg, B. Buttock, C. Thick Flank, D. Aitchbone.

Self-catering at 221B

"Tell me what kind of food you eat, and I will tell you what kind of man you are."

– Jean Anthelme Brillat-Savarin – 19th-century
French gastronome

When involved in a case, Mr. Holmes did not consume much nourishment – often going days without sustenance at all. This did not mean that he lacked appreciation for, or knowledge of, fine food. There were occasions, however, when dear Mr. Holmes (loathe to impose upon myself) would provide special catered gourmet dinners for himself, Dr. Watson and, occasionally, for visitors and clients. In fact, Mr. Holmes referred with some pride to his "merits as a housekeeper," which he believed Dr. Watson never quite appreciated.

Two adventures recounted by Dr. Watson mention dinners catered by Mr. Holmes: *The Sign of Four* and "The Noble Bachelor." In the former, he fêted the good doctor and Detective Inspector Athelney Jones. "It will be ready in half an hour," said Mr. Holmes. "I have oysters and a brace of grouse with something a little choice in white wines." The epicurean cold supper he served in "The Noble Bachelor" was described by Dr. Watson as "a couple of brace of cold woodcock, a pheasant, a pâté de fois gras pie, with a group of ancient and cobwebby bottles." It was delivered to 221B in a box. I shall expound on the subject of the pâté de fois gras pie presently.

Mr. Holmes could have obtained such lovely repasts at any number of places. Fortnum & Mason led a trend of providing luxury ready-to-eat foods, such as poultry and game in aspic all decorated and prepared to require no cutting. When Charles Dickens wrote about the Epsom Derby he said: "Look where I will...I see Fortnum & Mason. All the hampers fly open and burst into a blossom of lobster salad." Fortnum's is synonymous with out-of-household dining and also cater food to many men's clubs and large and small parties.

Wilton's, dating back to 1747, received its first Royal warrant as Purveyor of Oysters to Queen Victoria. Their catering services include dishes such as ballotine goose foie gras and goose foie gras en croute. Rules, one of the oldest restaurant in London, still flourishes and specializes in classic game cookery, oysters and pies – all available for home consumption. Chef Auguste Escoffier created many famous dishes at the Savoy Restaurant. One was his decadent fois gras dish, which he boasted as having the most expensive ingredients. These included one whole goose fois gras, which weighed two pounds and was wrapped in one pound of bacon, and baked inside puff pastry dough. All of these caterers are approximately two miles from 221B Baker Street.

In *The Sign of Four*, Mr. Holmes would have needed half an hour to plate his victuals and shuck, at minimum, 36 oysters — for the standard portion would be at least one dozen per diner.

As previously mentioned, dear Dr. Watson identified one dish in "The Noble Bachelor" adventure as a "pâté de fois gras pie." This dish, as stated, does not adhere to any known European recipe. (Note: Renowned Sherlockian Leslie S. Klinger provides an annotated entry on the subject and concludes that Dr. Watson was familiar with American cookery, where there exists such a dish and had therefore spent time in America.) In the French culinary lexicon, pâté originally meant the pastry casing of a filling — something akin to the translation "pastry-ed." Later, the filling itself became known as a "pâté" as well. All "pâtés" used to be baked in a crust and that was the distinction between pâtés en croute and pâtés en terrines (pâté filling served without a crust). The best English translation of pâtés en croute would be a "pâté pie." Hence, I believe Dr. Watson simply described the dish as it appeared to him, perhaps not knowing its correct French name. Mr. Holmes, having travelled to Paris and being of French decent, would most likely order the beautiful and rich pâté de fois gras en croute. Pâté is truly a French invention, patented in 1784, by Jean-Joseph Clause, chef to Louis XVI. Clause called his culinary invention "pâté de foie gras" or "pie of fat liver." The original recipe included 80 per cent fattened goose liver, which is still mandated by French law.

I confess I am astonished at the cost of oysters and foie gras today. Some oysters can fetch £3 each or more. As for goose liver, just one lobe weighing approximately two pounds is over £70. Then there is the hue and cry about the inhumane treatment of the goose, causing foie gras to be illegal in some locales. As game birds are still readily available, albeit at inflated prices, they are within reach of today's cooks. Pheasants, which are not native to Britain but originated in China, were brought to Rome and then to France and finally to England.

Recipes

Classic Terrine of Foie Gras – Makes 10 first course servings
Special equipment: 1 (3 - 4 cup) ceramic terrine, 3 inches deep (preferably oval with a lid); a piece of cardboard sized to fit just inside top of terrine, wrapped well in plastic wrap; and a 3-lb. weight (1 or 2 large soup cans). Terrine may last 3-5 days, kept

chilled in the mold with its surface covered with plastic wrap. Once unmolded, the terrine keeps, lightly wrapped in plastic wrap and chilled, another 3 days.

Ingredients: 1 (1 ½ -lb.) whole raw Grade A duck or goose foie gras at room temperature, cleaned and deveined, 4 tsp. kosher salt, ½ tsp. freshly ground white pepper, ¼ cup Sauternes or 3 Tbsp. Armagnac, toasted slices of dense sandwich loaf or baguette.

Mode: Preheat oven to 200F and line a small roasting pan with of folded kitchen towel or six layers of paper towels (this provides insulation so the bottom of the foie gras won't cook too quickly. Sprinkle each lobe and any loose pieces of foie gras on both sides with kosher salt and white pepper. Sprinkle 1/3 of Sauternes in terrine and firmly press large lobe of foie gras, smooth side down into the bottom (Wedge any loose pieces of foie gras into terrine to make lobe fit snugly). Sprinkle with another 1/3 of Sauternes. Put smaller lobe, smooth side up into terrine and press firmly down to create a flat surface and snug fit. Sprinkle with remaining Sauternes. Cover surface of foie gras with plastic wrap, then cover terrine with lid or foil. Put terrine (with plastic wrap and lid) in roasting pan and fill pan with enough hot water to reach halfway up side of terrine. Bake in middle of oven until an instant read thermometer inserted diagonally into centre of foie gras reaches 120F, 1 – 1 ½ hours or 160F (per USDA standards) about 3 ½ hours. Remove terrine from pan. Discard water and remove towel. Return terrine to roasting pan and remove lid. Put wrapped cardboard directly on surface of foie gras and set weight on cardboard (this will force fat to surface; don't worry if fat overflows.) Let stand at room temperature 20 minutes. Remove weight and cardboard and spoon any fat that dripped over side of terrine back onto top (fat will seal terrine). Chill, covered, until solid, at least 1 day. Unmold foie gras by running knife around edge. Invert onto a plate, fat side up, onto serving dish. Cut slices with heated sharp knife.

Game Pie — Note: if the game has been cooked in advance, and is put into pie when cold, allow slightly longer cooking time. The filling must be thoroughly heated through to boiling point. If you are uncertain about this, use a glass pie dish so that you can see what is happening.

Ingredients: 2-4 game birds, according to size (pheasant, grouse, partridge, woodpigeon), bouquet garni, stock or water, 1 large onion chopped, 8 oz. mushrooms sliced, 2 Tbsp. butter, 1 rounded Tbsp. flour, 6-8 slices of bacon (optional), 3-4 large hard-boiled eggs, quartered, salt, pepper and parsley, ½ lb. puff pastry, beaten egg for glazing.

Mode: For this recipe choose older birds or wood pigeons, rather than young roasting game. Put them into a pan with the bouquet and cover with stock or water plus salt and pepper. Simmer covered, until the meat begins to part from the bone, and can be cut away from the carcass in good-sized pieces. Arrange them in a pie dish. Brown the onions and mushrooms lightly in the butter – they should be golden rather than a deep brown. Stir in the flour and enough stock to make a rich, fairly thick but not gluey sauce. Simmer while you cut the bacon into convenient sized pieces for small rolls – these should be lightly grilled, then arranged around the meat, along with the pieces of hard-boiled eggs. Season with salt, pepper and chopped parsley. Pour over the onion and mushroom sauce which should come within half an inch of the top of the pie dish. Cover with the puff pastry. Brush over with beaten egg and bake for 30 minutes at 425F. The heat may be lowered once the pastry has risen well and is nicely browned.

SHEFFIELD CUTLERY & PLATE DIRECT FROM SHEFFIELD. [25 to 50 per cent. saved.]

"EDINBURGH" PATTERN.

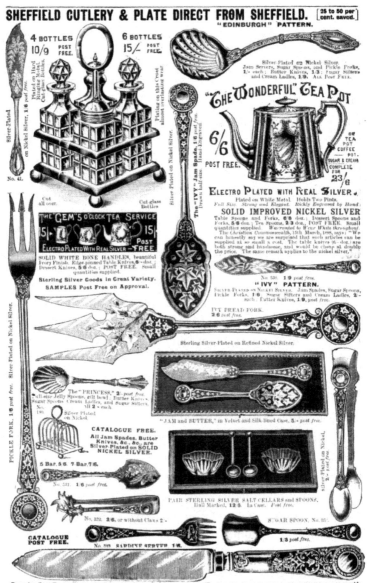

4 BOTTLES 10/9 POST FREE.

6 BOTTLES 15/- POST FREE.

Plated on Hard Ringing Metal. Cut-glass Bottles.

Silver-Plated on Nickel Silver.

No. 41.

Cut all over.

Cut-glass Bottles

Silver-Plated on Nickel Silver: Jam Servers, Sugar Spoons, and Pickle Forks, 1/- each; Butter Knives, 1/3; Sugar Sifters and Cream Ladles, 1/9. ALL POST FREE.

Silver Plated on Nickel Silver.

The "IVY" Jam Spade, 1/6 post free. Drawn half-size.

"THE WONDERFUL" TEA POT

6/6 POST FREE.

or TEA POT COFFEE POT.

SUGAR & CREAM COMPLETE FOR 23/6

ELECTRO PLATED WITH REAL SILVER.

Plated on White Metal. Holds Two Pints. Full Size. Strong and Elegant. Richly Engraved by Hand.

SOLID IMPROVED NICKEL SILVER

Table Spoons and Forks, 6/6 doz.; Dessert Spoons and Forks, 5/6 doz.; Tea Spoons, 2/3 doz., POST FREE. Small quantities supplied. Warranted to Wear White throughout. The Christian Commonwealth, 15th March, 1888, says: "We can honestly say we are surprised that such articles can be supplied at so small a cost. The table knives (6/- doz.) are both strong and handsome, and would be cheap at double the price. The same remark applies to the nickel silver."

No. 520. 1/9 post free.

"IVY" PATTERN.

SILVER-PLATED on NICKEL SILVER. Jam Spades, Sugar Spoons, Pickle Forks, 1/6; Sugar Sifters and Cream Ladles, 2/- each; Butter Knives, 1/9 post free.

IVY BREAD FORK. 2/6 post free.

The "GEM" 5 O'CLOCK TEA SERVICE 15/- 15/- ELECTRO PLATED WITH REAL SILVER—FREE. POST

SOLID WHITE BONE HANDLES, beautiful Ivory Finish. Edge-pinned Table Knives, 6/- doz.; Dessert Knives, 5/6 doz.; POST FREE. Small quantities supplied.

Sterling Silver Goods in Great Variety. SAMPLES Post Free on Approval.

Sterling Silver-Plated on Refined Nickel Silver.

The "PRINCESS," 2/- post free. Full-size Jelly Spoons, gilt bowl. Butter Knives, Sugar Spoons, Cream Ladles, and Sugar Sifters. No. 190. All 2/- each.

Silver Plated on Nickel.

CATALOGUE FREE. All Jam Spades, Butter Knives, &c., &c., are Silver-Plated on SOLID NICKEL SILVER.

"JAM and BUTTER," in Velvet and Silk-lined Case, 5/- post free.

5 Bar. 5/6. 7 Bar. 7/6.

No. 531. 1/6 post free.

CATALOGUE POST FREE.

No. 532. 2/6. or without Claw 2/-

PAIR STERLING SILVER SALT CELLARS and SPOONS, Hall Marked. 12/5. In Case. Post free.

Silver Plated on Nickel, 2/- post free.

PICKLE FORK. 1/6 post free. Silver Plated on Nickel Silver.

SUGAR SPOON. No. 93.

No. 533. SARDINE SERVER 1/6

1/3 post free.

Samples Post Free on Approval. Every Description of Cutlery and Plate. WM. CHEETHAM, Gent. Manager, to whom P.O.O.'s may be payable. ILLUSTRATED CATALOGUE FREE. Money returned or goods exchanged if not approved. Cheques crossed "Sheffield Union Bank." SHEFFIELD GOODS MANUFACTURING SUPPLY COMPANY, S Dept., Havelock Works, Young Street, SHEFFIELD.

36

Coffee in the Canon

"I'll light my spirit lamp, and give you a cup of coffee before we start."

–Sherlock Holmes in "The Golden Pince-Nez"

"The powers of a man's mind are directly proportioned to the quantity of coffee he drinks," so said Sir James Mackintosh (1765-1832), a Scottish jurist, politician and historian. This maxim could easily be applied to Mr. Holmes and Dr. Watson, since both often preferred coffee over tea throughout the day and into the night. A breakfast pot served hot and strong was mandatory. In Dr. Watson's account of *A Study in Scarlet* the first mention of coffee was made.

Dr. Watson "rose somewhat earlier than usual" and I was so accustomed to his sleeping in that he was dismayed that "his place had not been laid nor my coffee prepared. With the unreasonable petulance of mankind [he] rang the bell and gave the curt intimation that [he] was ready."

When Mr. Holmes worked relentlessly on a case, coffee served as a stimulant to both thinking and action, particularly after he stopped using cocaine. For Dr. Watson, who often lingered at various appointed locales to wait for Mr. Holmes, coffee served as a necessary pick-me-up, as seen in "The Naval Treaty." In this adventure a spirit lamp was employed by the station commissionaire to brew the necessary beverage. Many cases required night time activity and coffee was an ideal elixir. At 221B, I roasted and ground our own coffee.

Although England is regarded as a nation of tea drinkers, this was not always so. During the 17th and 18th centuries coffee was king: the English consumed 10 times as much coffee as tea. Over 2,000 coffee houses sprang up in London and attracted a variety of patrons, from doctors, merchants and writers to politicians. Runners went from coffee house to coffee house to relay information on major events of the day. On December 23, 1675, King Charles II made a proclamation to suppress coffee houses. Widespread citizen protests caused the rule to be revoked on January 8, 1676.

By the mid-1780s, however, tea made inroads due to pressure from the powerful British East India Company to cut import duties. Private traders who brought coffee from Britain's West Indian colonies did not wield as much political clout, so tea prices dropped and consumption increased. Tea was also easier to prepare – no roasting or grinding required. But the taste for coffee under the right circumstances remained.

I have noticed that many coffee shops are again appearing in London. Savory dishes now use coffee as an ingredient. It tenderizes and adds robust flavour and, like wine, coffee also has aromatic flavour notes — berries, caramel, cocoa, flora, nuts and spice. When added to savory recipes, coffee should be treated as a spice and freshly ground coffee is always preferable.

Recipes

Iced Coffee Mousse – Serves 2
Ingredients: 1/2 tsp. unflavored gelatin, 2 Tbsp. water, 1/2 cup sweetened condensed milk (not evaporated), 1 1/2 tsp. instant espresso powder, 1/2 tsp. vanilla, 1/2 cup well-chilled heavy cream.

Mode: In a small saucepan sprinkle the gelatin over the water and let it soften for 2 minutes. Add milk and espresso powder and heat the mixture over moderate heat, whisking constantly, until the powder is dissolved. Remove the pan from heat, stir in the vanilla, and set the pan in a bowl of ice and cold water, stirring the mixture every few minutes until it is thick and cold. In a small bowl beat the cream until it just holds stiff peaks and fold the coffee mixture into it gently but thoroughly. Spoon the mousse into 2 chilled long-stemmed glasses and chill until ready to serve.

Coffee Beef Stew– Serves 4

Ingredients: 2 Tbsp. extra-virgin olive oil; 1 ½ lbs. lean cubed stew beef; 2 onions, thinly sliced; 1 garlic clove, minced; 2 green bell peppers, halved, seeded, thickly sliced; ¼ cup all-purpose flour; 5 Tbsp. dry white wine; 5 Tbsp. strongly brewed coffee; salt and freshly ground pepper to taste; fresh thyme; bay leaves.

Mode: Heat oil in a large sauté pan over medium-high heat. Add meat and cook, stirring often, until browned on all sides. Remove meat and keep warm. Reduce heat to low and add onions, garlic and peppers, and cook over low heat, stirring often, for 10 minutes. Sprinkle in flour and cook, stirring continually, for 2 to 3 minutes. Gradually stir in wine and coffee. Increase heat to medium and bring to simmer, stirring constantly. Return the meat to the pan, season with salt and pepper to taste, add a few sprigs of fresh thyme, two bay leaves, cover and reduce heat to medium-low. Cover and simmer 1 hour or until meat is tender. Remove bay leaves and serve hot.

A cold collation

"You must be weary, for you've had a long day....said the lady as we entered a well-lit dining-room, upon the table of which a cold supper had been laid out......"

– Mrs. St. Clair in "The Man with the Twisted Lip."

"We shall have some cold supper before we start.."

– Sherlock Holmes in "Charles Augustus Milverton."

Late in the evening, often near the end of an elaborate social event, such as a ball or musicale, a fourth meal would be served to the guests. This meal, supper, or a "cold collation" was usually served around midnight, and was typically made up of a large selection of cold meats, fish and seafood, cheeses, bread and rolls, and perhaps some small savoury pastry creations, with a large selection of sweetmeats. It was presented in a highly formalized manner. *Mrs. Beeton's Book of Household Management* (published 1859-1861 in installments) presents two very specific diagrams for the dishes and placement of such for a cold collation. Her offerings include luxury items such as lobster and boar's head garnished with aspic jelly. There is also a representation for smaller celebrations.

If a family had gone out to the theatre for the evening, there would usually be a cold collation awaiting them upon their return home. Most gentlemen's clubs would put out a cold collation each evening around midnight for the refreshment of their members. In a fashionable home where guests were present, for the evening or at a house party, a cold supper was usually served, again near midnight.

When Mr. Holmes and Dr. Watson travelled at night to a destination or worked late into the night, they would often be served with a cold collation at a client's home. These cold suppers were simpler than those mentioned above, but nonetheless were carefully presented. Typically, these would be comprised of substantial fare: cold pies, sliced meats (tongue, ham and fowls were often included), salads and a selection of desserts. Cold poached salmon was a very popular dish for these suppers.

While the salads may have been simple– watercress, lettuce, celery and endive – the dressings were quite complex. There was a specialist, "The Fashionable Salad Maker," who could be engaged to provide appropriate dressings. This enterprising individual was a Frenchman named D'Albinac. Upon request, he or one of his many minions would show up with a mahogany chest which contained truffles, caviar, anchovies, ketchup and other aromatic ingredients. Cooks, too, often had their own specially guarded recipes for mayonnaise-based dressings, as well as access to commercially bottled options.

Everything offered at the table was sliced or presented in a manner that made it easy to help oneself to their choice of dishes. Jellies, *blanc mange*, trifle and tipsy cake (a sweet dessert cake, made from fresh sponge cakes soaked in sherry and brandy) were often offered as dessert options.

Garnishing cold collations became an art. Carrots and turnips were in the shapes of flowers while beetroots were cut into diamonds. Decorative skewers were threaded with aspic, cock's combs, mushrooms and shrimp and adorned cold meats whilst crystallized fruit, preserved violets and cherries were used to decorate jellies.

A 20th-century humourist, Terence Alan "Spike" Milligan, KBE, described the cold supper as: "The Dreaded Cold Collation: Small part of cold dead chicken...slice of tomato laid like wreath on dead chicken bit... thin slice of bread curling at edges as though about to fly off plate... six pale peas glued together for security ....."

Recipes

Cold Poached Salmon with Green Mayonnaise – Serves 6-8
Ingredients: 2-3 lb. cut of salmon tail end, skin on; 5 heaping Tbsp. salt, 1 tsp. good vinegar, salt and pepper to taste, 1 large egg, ¼ cup chopped chives, 2 sprigs fresh tarragon, ½ cup chopped fresh parsley, 1 medium clove of garlic, 1 cup olive oil, 1 Tbsp. sour cream.

Mode: Place salmon in pot then cover with cold water. Add salt and bring to boil. Turn off immediately and let salmon sit in hot water for 30 minutes. Remove fish from water and chill. To make mayonnaise, put vinegar, salt, pepper, egg, chives, tarragon, parsley, garlic and 1 Tbsp. oil in food processor or blender. Process 10 seconds then slowly add remainder of oil in very thin stream. The mayonnaise is done when all the oil is added and is creamy thick. Taste for seasoning and mix in sour cream. Mayonnaise will keep for at least a week when chilled. To serve salmon remove skin with fork and debone using spoon. Serve mayonnaise in separate dish.

Fruit and Wine Jelly – Serves 6
Ingredients: 1 lb. 6oz fresh raspberries, ¾ cup sugar, 1 ¼ cup medium dry white wine, 5 sheets gelatine or 6 if to be set out in a mould.

Mode: Put raspberries and sugar in pan with scant ½ cup water. Heat gently until the fruit releases juices and becomes very soft and sugar dissolved. Remove from heat and tip into fine sieve lined with cheesecloth and leave to drain into large bowl (this will take time but do not squeeze berries). When juice has drained make it up to 2 ½ cups with water if needed. Soak gelatine in cold water 5 minutes to soften. Heat ½ the juice until very hot but not boiling. Remove from heat. Squeeze gelatine to remove excess water, then stir into hot juice until dissolved. Stir in remaining juice and wine. Pour into stemmed glasses or wetted mould and chill until set.

COLD COLLATION DISHES.

1—Pigeon Pie. 2—Raised Game Pie. 3—Cutlets and Peas. 4—Prawns en Bouquet. 5—Crème Chicken, 6—Plovers' Eggs. 7—Lamb Cutlets. 8—Larks Farcie. 9—Piped Ham. 10—Boned Capon.

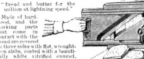

Mrs. Hudson's
"Three Pipe Problem"

"You don't mind the smell of strong tobacco I hope."

– Sherlock Holmes in *A Study in Scarlet*

There are times, I admit, that I wished Sir Frances Drake never brought tobacco to England in 1573. My dear lodgers were quite addicted to the substance. Even Dr. Watson, a heavy smoker himself, referred to Mr. Holmes as a "self-poisoner by cocaine and tobacco" in "The Adventure of the Five Orange Pips."

It is a known fact that the exchequer made considerable revenue from taxing tobacco in the early days. In 1614 it was estimated that there were over 7,000 tobacco shops in London. By 1619 King James I proclaimed that all tobacco must enter the country via London and that pipes be made by a group of pipe-makers in Westminster. This group was re-incorporated by Charles I in 1634 and eventually became known today as The Worshipful Company of Tobacco Pipe Makers and Pipe blenders.

I previously mentioned the large number of coffee houses that existed in the early part of the 18th century and these also catered to the tobacco smoking public as well. Simpsons in the Strand began in 1828 as a chess club and coffee house known as "The Grand Cigar Divan." The main restaurant today is still known as The Great Divan.

Mr. Holmes found that the study of tobacco ashes provided vital knowledge in his work, and wrote a monograph on the subject titled "Upon the Distinction between the Ashes of the Various Tobaccos." In "The Boscombe Valley Mystery," he claimed that through this work he was able to distinguish between any brand of cigarette, tobacco or cigar. Indeed, in the matter of pipes he believed they expressed "more individuality save for watches and bootlaces."

The tobacco house frequented by Dr. Watson and Mr. Holmes was Bradley's. Dr. Watson used a Ship's blend early on and later switched to an Acadia mixture, whilst Mr. Holmes favoured Shag tobacco. Today's Shag is a very finely shredded tobacco used primarily in rolling cigarettes. Mr. Holmes's shag was more coarsely cut and was considered to be a strong tobacco of a less-desirable quality. Whilst it is recommended that tobacco be kept in an airtight container, Mr. Holmes preferred a Persian slipper to hold his pipe blend. Cigars were higher quality Cubans but Mr. Holmes eschewed a humidor for the coal scuttle. He stored his pipes on his bedroom mantle. His favourite pipes being a blackened clay which he used when in a contemplative mood, an oily briar that I recall having an amber stem, and a cherry wood. His cigarettes were made by his tobacconist and were carried in a metal case. On occasion, he used snuff taken from a beautiful gold case with a large amethyst stone given to him in gratitude by the King of Bohemia. Each day Mr. Holmes saved the leavings of his pipes in a heap on my lovely mantelpiece only to smoke them the next morning. This unusual frugality confounded me.

Often the sitting room would be shrouded as a London pea souper with the blue smoke from Mr. Holmes's pipe as he contemplated a challenging case. He would often call such situations "a three pipe problem." Dr. Watson wrote in "The Adventure of the Red-Headed League" that Mr. Holmes: "curled himself up in his chair, with his knees drawn up to his hawklike nose, and there he sat with his eyes closed and his black clay pipe thrusting out like the bill of some strange bird." Indeed, he often smoked as much as an ounce at a time, as documented in "The Man with the Twisted Lip."

There were also occasions when Mr. Holmes's dry sense of humour about smoking was evident. In "The Veiled Lodger" he commented to Dr. Watson that "Mrs. Merrilow does not object to tobacco, Watson, if you wish to indulge your filthy habit."

But their heavy smoking posed many difficulties for me and my maids with the upkeep of their rooms. I frequently had to have the decorators in to paint their rooms whilst they were away on a prolonged case. Considerable care had to be taken so as not to upset the rather unorthodox manner in which they lived. I had to devise methods of cleaning furniture and soft materials. For wood, the cane chair and other hard surfaces such as brass and glass, soapy, hot water was swished to make a great volume of suds. (Your washing-up liquid available today would do nicely.) Dip a cloth only in the foam and apply vigorously. Rinse with a cloth moistened in clear water. Then wipe dry with a clean cloth and wax or polish as required. For curtains and other washable fabrics such as antimacassars, I made a solution of warm water, soap and vinegar and soaked the item for 15 minutes. They were then rinsed with fresh water. Any remaining stains were sponged with rubbing alcohol. One more good rinse was required. The items were allowed to dry and laundered as soon as possible. One almost had to be quite as good a chemist as Mr. Holmes to keep the rooms clean so that visiting clients were not overcome with the results of tobacco consumption.

Recipes

Smoker's Coffee – serves 2

Ingredients: ¼ cup green crème de menthe, ¼ cup Tia Maria or Kahlua, 1 ½ cups hot strong coffee, ¼ cup heavy cream, whipped, 2 "After 8" square or long style chocolates

Mode: Divide the two liquors equally between two tall glasses (preferably with handles). Fill each glass equally with coffee. Top each glass with whipped cream. Garnish with After 8 squares cut diagonally or two long-style chocolates.

Tobacco Cookies – makes 24

Preheat the oven to 355°F. Line a baking sheet with parchment paper.

Ingredients: Tobacco Coconut Flakes: 1 cup firmly packed sweetened coconut flakes, 1 ½ cups brewed coffee, ¾ cup cola, 2 tsp. molasses, 2 Tbsp. sugar, 2 Tbsp. Tobacco Water (recipe follows). Cookies: 1 ¼ cups all-purpose flour, ¼ tsp. baking powder, pinch of salt, 14 oz. semisweet chocolate, chopped; 2 Tbsp. unsalted butter, 2 large eggs, 1/3 cup sugar, 1 Tbsp. buttermilk, 1 tsp. vanilla extract, 2 tsp. chopped tobacco leaves (reserved from cigar used to make Tobacco Water). Tobacco Water: 1 good mild cigar, 3 cups warm water

Mode: To make the tobacco water, peel half of the layers off the cigar and discard. Separate the inner tobacco leaves. Reserve 2 Tbsp. worth of chopped leaves to use in cookies; set aside. Rinse remaining leaves under warm water for three minutes. Fill a small bowl with the three cups warm water and steep the tobacco leaves in the water for 10 minutes. Strain the water and discard the tobacco leaves. The tobacco water will be quite strong, with a nicotine sting.

To make the coconut flakes: In a medium saucepan combine the coconut, coffee, cola, molasses, sugar and tobacco water. Bring to a boil over high heat and boil for about 20 minutes, until all the liquid has been cooked off. Transfer the coconut flakes to a baking sheet and allow to cool to room temperature.

To make the cookies: In a small bowl, combine the flour, baking powder and salt and stir together with a fork. Melt the chocolate and butter over a double boiler. Allow to cool slightly. In a separate bowl, whisk together the eggs, sugar, buttermilk, vanilla and tobacco. Stir into the chocolate mixture, then stir the flour mixture into this batter. Spoon the dough 1 Tbsp. at a time onto the prepared baking sheet. Leave room in between for the cookies to spread while baking. Top each cookie with a little of the tobacco coconut flakes. Bake for 10 to 12 minutes, until the cookie tops crack but the cookies are still soft in the centre. Let cool for three minutes before handling. Lift with a spatula and transfer the cookies to a wire rack. Let cool completely and store in an airtight container for up to a week.

Tobacco Onions – Named as such because they resemble tobacco leaves
Ingredients: 3 large white onions (2 lbs.), halved lengthwise and very thinly sliced crosswise; 2 cups whole milk, 2 cups all-purpose flour, ¼ cup plus 2 Tbsp. smoked paprika, 2 ½ Tbsp. celery salt, 2 ½ quarts canola or vegetable oil, Kosher salt.

Mode: In a large bowl, combine the onions with the milk and stir to coat. Cover and refrigerate for two hours. In a medium bowl, whisk the flour with the paprika and celery salt. Drain the onions very well in a colander, then set the colander over a large bowl. Sprinkle the flour mixture over the onions and toss with your hands to evenly coat. Shake well to remove any excess flour. In a large saucepan, heat the oil to 350°. In about five batches, fry the onions over moderate heat until golden brown, about two minutes per batch. Using a slotted spoon, transfer the onions to paper towels to drain; season lightly with salt. Return the oil to 350F between batches. Serve hot.

" HOLMES OPENED IT AND SMELLED THE SINGLE
CIGAR WHICH IT CONTAINED."

Prince of Wales soup

A pot of nourishing and hearty soup is usually kept simmering in my kitchen. It is an ideal meal for Mr. Holmes and Dr. Watson in cold, wet weather and suits their unpredictable schedules. Here is a soup I favour for it is frugal and named for our future king. It was included in *Mrs. Beeton's Book of Household Management*, first published in 1861. This was the first cookery book to list ingredients, preparation time, method, average cost, seasonality and number of servings. I refer to it often.

"This soup was invented...to be distributed among the poor when the Prince of Wales attains his majority on 9 November 1859.... The best wish we can offer the young prince is that in his own path he may ever keep before him the bright example of his royal mother and show himself worthy of her name. There are few in these realms who will not give a fervent response to these sentiments."

—Mrs. Beeton's Book of Household Management

Queen Victoria held "Bertie" responsible for the death of her beloved consort Albert. Relations between mother and son were strained at best. Albert Edward, Prince of Wales, became King Edward VII in 1901 when he was 60.

– David Williamson: *History of the Kings and Queens of England*, Kronecky&Kronecky, (2008).

Recipes

Prince of Wales Soup – Time 2 hours. Seasonable in winter. Sufficient for 6 persons
Ingredients: 12 turnips, 1 lump of sugar, 2 spoonfuls of strong veal stock, salt and white pepper to taste, 2 quarts of very bright stock

Mode: Peel turnips and with a cutter, cut them in balls as round as possible but very small. Put them in the stock, which must be very bright, and simmer until tender. Add the veal stock and seasonings. Have little pieces of bread cut round, about the size of a shilling; moisten them with stock; put them into a tureen and pour the soup over without shaking, for fear of crumbling the bread, which would spoil the appearance of the soup and make it look thick.

London Particular Soup– Serves 4-6
Another hearty soup that I favour is this "London Particular Soup" which was named after London fogs which were known as "pea soupers" or "London Particular":

Ingredients: 1 ½ cups dried split yellow or green peas, 2 Tbsp. butter, 6 strips bacon finely chopped, 1 medium onion finely chopped, 1 medium carrot thinly sliced, 1 celery stick thinly sliced, 7 ½ cups chicken stock, 4 Tbsp. heavy cream, salt and ground black pepper, croutons or fried crumbled bacon to serve.

Mode: Put split peas into large bowl, cover well with boiling water (from the kettle) and leave to stand. Meanwhile, melt butter in a large, sturdy pot. Add bacon, onion, carrot and celery and cook over medium heat for 10-15 minutes, stirring occasionally until the vegetables are soft and beginning to turn golden brown. Drain the peas and add them to the pan. Stir in the stock. Bring back to a boil and simmer gently for about one hour or until the peas are very soft. Season to taste and add cream. Heat until just bubbling and serve with croutons and pieces of crumbled bacon on top.

BOVRIL

Unequalled as a Winter Beverage.

Unsurpassed for Culinary Purposes.

Undoubtedly the most Perfect Food known.

Invaluable to Invalids and Weak Persons.

BOVRIL

Travel Outerwear Part 1 — Victorian maxim: "Let the clothing suit the occasion"

"If people turn to look at you on the street, you are not well dressed."

– Beau Brummel

George Bryan 'Beau' Brummell established the mode of dress for men that rejected overly ornate fashions for one of understated but perfectly fitted and bespoke (custom-tailored) garments. This look was based on dark coats, full-length trousers rather than knee breeches and stockings, and above all, immaculate shirt linen and an elaborately knotted cravat. Brummell is credited

with introducing, and establishing as fashion, the modern men's suit, worn with a necktie. He claimed he took five hours a day to dress, and recommended that boots be polished with champagne.

Mr. Holmes and Dr. Watson were always impeccably dressed and had all their attire custom-made. The only exception was Mr. Holmes's unfortunate "mouse coloured" dressing gown. ("The Bruce Partington Plans" and "The Empty House"). He wore this robe most often between cases as it suited his rather morose mood at those times. Mr. Holmes had two more presentable dressing gowns: blue ("The Man with a Twisted Lip"), and purple ("The Blue Carbuncle").

Formal evening dress consisted of a frock coat, plain or narrow pinstripe straight trousers with a dark waistcoat, white bow tie, a shirt with a winged collar, and high top hat (which was also worn in daytime by many gentlemen, including Mr. Holmes). Gentlemen out for an evening's formal entertainment, for example, attending the opera or symphony, may wear a dark cape with a silk or satin lining. Walking canes were often highly decorative. For Mr. Holmes, an expert practitioner of single-stick fighting, canes were also highly functional ("The Illustrious Client").

Daytime attire was similar to evening wear, save for a dark tie or a fine Harris Tweed lounge suit. Bowler hats in winter were an option to the tall hat. Knee length topcoats, often with contrasting trim, velvet or fur collars, or calf-length overcoats were worn in winter. In summer, light-coloured, lightweight trousers and a boater (straw hat with ribbon band) were seen. Men's city boots and dress pumps generally had built-up heels and a narrow toe. Mr. Holmes' bootmaker undoubtedly contributed to impressions of Mr. Holmes being of greater height than his six feet.

Savile Row, a street in London, was considered the "golden mile" of bespoke tailoring. Nearby Jermyn and Bond Streets were noted for fine haberdashery. Mr. Holmes and Dr. Watson frequently sought refreshment when in the area day or night at the convenient and excellent Grand Café Royal on Regent Street. Mr. Holmes was accosted outside it by roughs who escaped through the restaurant and out into the street behind it ("The Illustrious Client"). In 1894, the night porter of the Grand Café Royal was found with two bullets in his head. The case was never solved.

Recipes from the Grand Café Royal Menu

Caille en Casserole

Ingredients: 8-12 quail, salt, flour, ⅓ cup butter, ½ lb. Fresh mushrooms, chopped fresh parsley, dry white wine — about 2 cups.

Mode: Split the birds down the back. Salt and dust lightly in flour. Sauté in skillet until browned on both sides. Remove quail from skillet and place in a casserole with lid. Pour drippings from skillet over birds, add mushrooms and parsley. Pour enough wine into casserole to half-cover the birds. Cover and place in 350F oven for one hour. (Doves and quarters of pheasant may also be done this way. Allow only 45 minutes in oven for doves and 1¼ hours for pheasant.)

Carréd'Agneau au Sauce Menthe

Ingredients: Three 8-chop racks of lamb, 6 Tbsp. Dijon mustard, 3 cups fresh white breadcrumbs, 6 Tbsp. chopped fresh mint, salt and pepper.

Mode: Preheat oven to 450F. Sprinkle lamb with salt and pepper. Spread 1 Tbsp. mustard on each side of each lamb rack. Mix breadcrumbs and mint in medium bowl. Press onto lamb, coating completely. Arrange lamb, meat side up, on large baking sheet. Roast lamb 10 minutes. Reduce oven temperature to 350F. Roast until lamb registers 130F for rare, or medium-rare 20 minutes longer. Tent with parchment (or foil); let stand five minutes. Cut lamb racks between bones into chops. Arrange on plates. Garnish with mint sprigs; pass Sauce Menthe (recipe below) separately.

Sauce Menthe– Yield: 1 Cup

Ingredients: 2 cups good quality white wine vinegar, ¾ cup sugar, ½ cup finely chopped fresh mint leaves.

Mode: In heavy-bottomed saucepan, combine sugar and vinegar. Bring to a boil over medium heat, then lower to simmer and cook until the liquid is reduced by half, 10 to 12 minutes. It should be thick and syrupy. Remove from heat and cool five minutes. Add mint leaves. Stir, then pour into a bowl. Cover the bowl, let it sit for about an hour like steeping a cup of tea. Serve at room temperature. Yield: 1 C. Sauce Menthe.

Travel Outerwear Part 2— Victorian maxim: "Let the clothing suit the occasion"

Approximately half of the published adventures of Mr. Holmes occurred outside of London. Travel was often undertaken on extremely short notice. Both Mr. Holmes and Dr. Watson travelled lightly, often with a single satchel. Gentlemen were always appropriately turned out for first-class train travel. Mr. Paget's illustrations for *The Strand* magazine depict the travel attire of my lodgers in "The Boscombe Valley Mystery" and "Silver Blaze." If Mr. Holmes had objections to the illustrations in the first story, he would have no compunction about expressing his complaints, and having them addressed in the second.

Coats — The travelling coat preferred by Dr. Watson was the Wellesley, made of heavy wool. It was available in both long and knee lengths, with or without velvet collars. He wore the short coat in London and the long style for travel. Mr. Holmes selected the Ulster (also known as Inverness). A genuine Ulster is made of Donegal Tweed from Donegal County in the province of Ulster. The coat had a detachable hood and cape. To express the informal character of the coat, it had patch pockets and contrast stitching along the edges and cuffs. The Ulster was cut generously and could appear bulky if it hadn't a back "half belt" with adjustable buttons to change the degree of the waist suppression. In the illustrations for both mentioned stories, Mr. Holmes wears the Ulster without the optional cape.

Hats — The good doctor favoured a bowler derby for travel and would occasionally trade it for a boater in summer. I would like to

state unequivocally that dear Mr. Holmes did indeed often wear a deerstalker hat in his travels – but never, ever in London, where it would have been a serious *faux pas*. In "Boscombe Valley," he is described by Dr. Watson as sporting "the familiar close-fitting, ear-flapped, cloth travelling cap." As the deerstalker was the most typical cap of the period matching both descriptions, it is not surprising that the original illustrations for the stories by Mr. Paget depicted Holmes as a "deerstalker man." The only other close-fitting cloth cap of the period was the single-front brim style worn by golfers, workmen or newsboys, and lacking the distinctive earflaps. The deerstalker was distinguished by its dual visors and a pair of unstiffened cloth flaps attached to either side of the cap. These were tied together by grosgrain ribbons or laces. The earflaps, tied under the chin, provided protection in cold weather and high winds while the dual visors offered sun protection. Deerstalkers may be made of solid-coloured material but were most often found with hound's-tooth check, herringbone or plaid patterns.

Here are two recipes from Devonshire, which was the setting for "Silver Blaze." They were commonly served at the local public houses, inns and hotels.

Recipes

Devon Crab Soup– Serves 4-6

Ingredients: 2 Tbsp. butter, 1 medium onion and 1 celery stalk finely chopped, 1 garlic clove crushed, 1 ½ Tbsp. flour, 8 oz. cooked crab meat, 5 cups fish stock, ⅔ cup heavy cream, 2 Tbsp. dry sherry, salt and pepper.

Mode: Melt butter in a pan and add onion, celery and garlic. Cook over medium heat five minutes, stir frequently until the vegetables are soft but not brown. Remove from heat and quickly stir in the flour and ½ of the crab. Gradually stir in stock. Bring just to a boil, reduce heat and simmer 30 minutes. Purée the soup and return to cleaned pan. Season to taste with salt and pepper. Chop remaining crab and stir into pan with the cream and sherry. Reheat soup and serve immediately.

Devonshire Chicken Dumplings – Serves 4-6

Ingredients: 8 oz. cooked chicken, 2 fried chicken livers, 2 fried slices streaky bacon, 2 cups dry bread crumbs, 2 large eggs lightly beaten, salt and pepper, 2 sprigs chopped parsley, flour, 3-4 cups chicken stock, 2 egg yolks lightly beaten, ⅔ cup cream, ½ cup grated cheese, chopped parsley for garnish.

Mode: Mince chicken, livers and bacon together and mix with breadcrumbs, eggs, salt, pepper and parsley. Roll into balls the size of walnuts and sprinkle with flour. Over low heat, simmer them in chicken stock for 12-15 minutes. Remove to heatproof dish and keep warm. For sauce, combine yolks, cream and 1¼ cups of cooking liquid. Season to taste and simmer without boiling. Pour sauce over dumplings, sprinkle with cheese and brown under hot grill. Serve immediately, sprinkled with parsley.

Devonshire Junket – Serves 4

Ingredients: 2 ½ cups of whole unhomogenized milk, 3 Tbsp. superfine sugar, several drops of triple-strength rosewater, 2 tsp. rennet, 4 Tbsp. heavy cream, sugared rose petals to decorate (optional).

Mode: Gently heat the milk with 2 Tbsp. of the superfine sugar, stirring, until the sugar has dissolved and the temperature reaches 98.4F. Remove from heat and stir in rosewater to taste and then the rennet. Pour the junket into serving dishes and leave undisturbed at room temperature for two to three hours, until set. Do not move during this time, otherwise it will separate into curds and whey. Stir the remaining sugar into the cream, then carefully spoon the mixture over the surface of the set junket. Decorate with sugared rose petals if you wish.

The dining car

"Science, as illustrated by the printing press, the telegraph, the railway, is a double-edged sword. At the same moment that it puts an enormous power in the hands of the good man, it also offers an equal advantage to the evil disposed."

— Writer, John Richard Jefferies (1848-1887)

Travel by train was either mentioned or used in 41 of the adventures of Dr. Watson and Mr. Holmes. Although Holmes kept a copy of *Bradshaw's Railway Guide* on his mantle at 221B, he knew the timetables virtually by heart. Charing Cross (which was located in the west end and thus closest to Baker Street) figured in six adventures, while Waterloo, Victoria and Paddington were each mentioned in five. The train-de-luxe, mentioned in "The Adventure of the Mazarin Stone," was a French train composed entirely of first-class or Pullman carriages.

Railway travel permitted the good Doctor and Holmes time to read, talk and eat in comfort as they pursued their cases. In short, it was a practical, speedy conveyance without much inconvenience. As the Jefferies quote above implies, Professor Moriarty also used the trains and employed a "special train" for his trip to Meiringen in "The Final Problem."

In the early days of train travel, the food provided was not always up to par. Just before Britain's first dining car took to the rails, novelist Anthony Trollope (1815-1882) wrote that the "real disgrace of England is the railway sandwich." Food used to be supplied at stops *en route* and was often cold and unpalatable.

The very first meal to be served on a train was in 1874 on the Midland Rail Service. In 1879, the Great Northern Railway outfitted a fully equipped and beautifully appointed Pullman car, named the Prince of Wales, as a full-service dining car that served meals cooked and prepared *en route*. It is not known if the Prince of Wales himself ever enjoyed a meal while in the carriage named after him but rumour has it that he did.

Other railway lines followed this example and spared no expense in creating the most luxurious and elegant train dining cars so that passengers could enjoy a fine-dining experience. The foods served on railroads, always accompanied by champagne, equaled that of the finest restaurants, hotels and steamships. Most of the better railroads served meals on bone china plates embossed with the company's own crest. These pieces often depicted scenes along the train's route.

Lunch aboard the train in Victorian times would have been a five-course affair, with dishes such as grilled turbot, roast sirloin, salmon with hollandaise sauce, soufflé, bread-and-butter pudding, treacle tart and crème caramel. The cost in 1898 was half a crown — about £10 in today's money. The early waiters learned their trade by being taught to walk along a white line wearing a blindfold whilst the train moved at speed.

The modern later years, after privatization, were not kind to the restaurant cars. A tradition that lasted almost 150 years of fine dining on the move was mostly ended; replaced by a concession stand or trolleys offering pre-made victuals. One of the only places where the experience has survived is on the London to the West Country, and Swansea trains. These routes have proved so popular that First Great Western has recently started adding more scheduled trains with thoughts of expansion to other routes as well.

Recipes

Treacle Tart – Makes 9" pie
Preheat oven to 350F.

Ingredients: 1½ cups English Golden Syrup or ¾ cup light and ¾ cup dark corn syrup, 1½ cup fresh breadcrumbs, 1 Tbsp. lemon juice, ½ tsp. ground ginger, 2 large eggs, 9" unbaked pie shell. Garnish with whipped cream, custard sauce or ice cream.

Mode: Combine syrup, breadcrumbs, lemon juice, ginger and eggs in large bowl. Mix well. Pour into pie shell and bake for 20-25 minutes. The tart should be golden brown when done.

Turbot en Papillote– Serves 4
May substitute cod, halibut, haddock, sole, flounder.

Preheat oven to 450F.

Cut out four 12" squares of parchment paper or aluminum foil.

Ingredients: 2 slivered garlic cloves, four 4-6 oz. pieces of turbot fillet or steaks, salt and pepper to taste, 8 thick slices beefsteak tomato, 8 fresh basil leaves, 2 Tbsp. pine nuts, 1 Tbsp. olive oil

Mode: Place a bit of garlic on each square of parchment; top each with a piece of fish, salt and pepper, two slices tomato, two basil leaves, some pine nuts and the barest drizzle of olive oil. Place sealed packages of fish in a large baking dish and back about 30 minutes. The fish should be white, opaque and tender. Serve closed packages individually.

FISH.

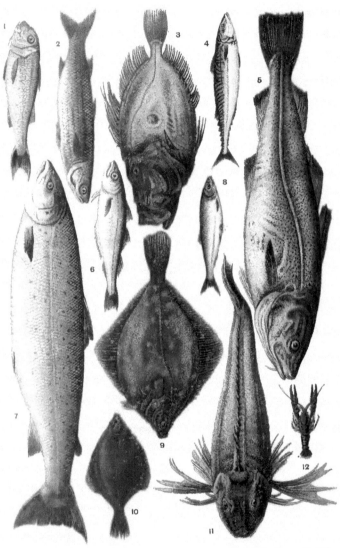

1.—Red Mullet.　2.—Grayling.　3.—John Dory.　4.—Mackerel.　5.—Cod.
6.—Whiting.　7.—Salmon.　8.—Herring.　9.—Plaice.　10.—Flounder.　11.—Gurnet.
12.—Crayfish.

At Claridge's

"You can report to me in London to-morrow, Martha, at Claridge's Hotel."

— Sherlock Holmes in "His Last Bow"

The venerable Claridge's hotel appeared in two of Dr. Watson's accounts of his cases with Mr. Holmes: "His Last Bow" and "Thor Bridge" in which Mr. Gibson, the former U.S. senator and "the greatest gold mining magnate in the world," stayed whilst in London. The hotel was well known to Mr. Holmes as he had dined in its remarkable restaurant many times with renowned clients. It is conveniently located on Brook Street in Mayfair, only a 15-minute walk from Baker Street.

Claridge's opened in 1812. Operating first under the name Mivart's Hotel, it attracted the wealthy and royal even during its early period. Prior to his ascension to the throne, King George IV had a suite permanently reserved there. As the success of Mivart's grew, so did the physical dimensions of the hotel. At the same time, William and Marianne Claridge were running their own successful hotel on Brook Street. They purchased Mivart's in 1854. The two merged properties were then known as Claridge's, late Mivart's until 1856 when it became simply Claridge's.

The hotel's reputation continued to rise. In 1860, Empress Eugénie of France made Claridge's her winter home. She invited Queen Victoria and Prince Albert to dine with her there and they were delighted with it. By the 1880s, Claridge's was referred to as "the extension to Buckingham Palace" and it seemed everyone in the *Almanach de Gotha*, a directory of Europe's royalty and higher nobility, visited. As a result, the hotel continued to have a steady stream of visiting royalty.

The Savoy Hotel's owner, Richard D'Oyly Carte, bought Claridge's in 1894, gutted the old buildings and replaced them with modern hotel facilities, lifts and *en suite* bathrooms. The refurbished hotel reopened in 1898 with 203 rooms and suites.

The Ritz, The Savoy, Grosvenor House and London's other grand hotels may compete with it in opulence, but none can hold a candle to Claridge's when it comes to richness of history, its wonderful food and magnificence of clientele. The Chef, Edouard Nignon, was the former chef de cuisine to the Czar of Russia and the Emperor of Austria. He held his post at Claridge's from 1894 - 1901.

The following recipe comes from Claridge's December 22, 1898 menu. *Hors d'oeuvres a la Russe* were offered because of the many Russian guests. This is an assortment of small plates of delicacies, including blinis and caviar, *oeuffs à la Russe* and smoked sturgeon. The hors d'oeuvres also had sparkling aspics, richly decorated pâtés, elaborate butter rosettes and carved vegetable flowers.

Recipes

Oeuffs à la Russe – Serves 6
Ingredients: 6 hard-boiled eggs cut in half lengthwise, yolks removed, reserve egg whites, 2 Tbsp. mayonnaise, crème fraiche or sour cream; ½ tsp. mustard powder; 1 Tbsp. Dijon mustard; 2 finely chopped green onions or 3 Tbsp. finely chopped chives; salt & pepper to taste. *Garnish*: caviar or capers and a pinch of paprika.

Mode: mix all ingredients together and pipe or stuff into egg whites. Add garnish on top of each stuffed egg. Serve on lettuce leaves.

Buckwheat Blinis – Serves 10 as an appetizer

Ingredients: 1 ¾ cups whole milk, 2 tsp. sugar, 1 package dry active yeast, ¾ cup buckwheat flour, ¾ cup all-purpose flour, ½ tsp. salt, 3 Tbsp. unsalted melted butter, 2 Tbsp. vegetable oil, plus additional for frying, 3 large egg yolks, 2 large egg whites, 1 small potato halved.

Mode: In a small saucepan scald the milk over low heat. Transfer to a large bowl and cool until lukewarm (105-115F). Add 1 tsp. sugar and the yeast to milk, stir and let stand until foamy, about five minutes. Whisk in the buckwheat and all-purpose flours, salt, remaining sugar, butter, 2 Tbsp. vegetable oil and the egg yolks until smooth. Let rise in warm place, covered, until doubled in bulk, about one hour. In a separate bowl, beat the egg whites until they form stiff peaks and fold into the batter. Dip the potato half in oil and rub over the bottom of a large, non-stick skillet. Heat the pan over medium heat for one minute. Drop the batter by tablespoonful into the skillet, spacing one inch apart. Cook until the undersides are golden, about one minute. Turn and cook 30 seconds more. Transfer to heatproof plate. Repeat with the remaining batter, greasing the skillet with the oiled potato before each batch. Keep the cooked blini covered with foil in a 275F oven.

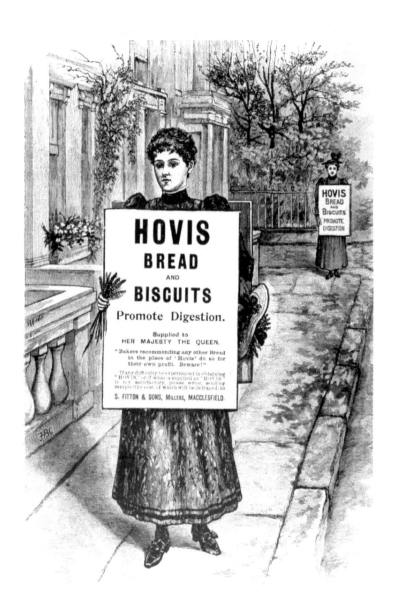

Dining at Baskerville Hall

"Surely you will stay and have some dinner."

– Sir Henry Baskerville in *The Hound of the Baskervilles*.

Dr. Watson noted that the dining room at Baskerville Hall was a place of "shadow and gloom" since the death of Sir Charles, but he also referred to the room as a "banqueting hall" and hence more commodious and sumptuous than most formal dining rooms. After young Sir Henry spent time on the Continent recovering from his ordeal he no doubt would return Baskerville Hall to its rightful place as a well-run baronial home. That would also indicate he was prepared to entertain guests in a style reflecting his position in society. He would need to replace the Barrymores and add a full complement of servants. As Mrs. Beeton states in *Mrs. Beeton's Book of Household Management*: "To invite a person to your house is to take charge of his happiness so long as he is beneath you roof." Sir Henry indubitably would adopt that philosophy. The following is a description of a dinner party for 12 – the ideal number of guests in my time – which Sir Henry could have at Baskerville Hall.

Until Victorian times, dinner was presented *á la française*, with all the courses set out at the same time. Dining style then changed to *à la russe* service – where the dishes were served individually by footmen on platters and cleared before the next course as directed by the butler. The butler watched over the host's shoulder to determine how the dinner progressed and worked with the cook to time when to remove dishes and when to serve the next course. Accompanying the main meal were often 12 kickshaws – appetizers and side dishes designed to fill empty places on the table. Dinner parties provided the opportunity to display wealth since they required many staff, elaborate table settings and many delicacies. A highly decorative floral centerpiece often graced the table.

Mrs. Beeton provides several dinner party menus for 12. The first course begins with soups: one clear and one thick. Soups were regarded as the keynote of the dinner because they revealed the calibre of the cook. This was followed by fish dishes, which often featured a whole boiled turbot in lobster sauce. Entrees for the first course might include chicken patties, sweetbreads, filet of beef and rissoles, or small sweet or savory pastries. The second course was replete with a joint or saddle of meat, roast fillet of veal with béchamel sauce, roast fowls stuffed with truffles, and vegetables and boiled ham. It was fashionable to next serve a sorbet. The third course included game birds such as ducklings or guinea fowl, meringues, orange jelly, macaroni with Parmesan cheese, tarts and lobster salad to round out the vast dinner.

Finally, desserts, ices, fruit and cheeses were presented. Mrs. Beeton noted that "it may be said, that 'if there be any poetry at all in meals...there is poetry in the dessert'...." She also states that "...chocolate in different forms is indispensable to our desserts."

Recipes

Chocolate Soufflé
Ingredients: 4 large eggs, 3 tsp. sugar, 1tsp. flour, 3 oz. of the best chocolate, finely grated.

Mode: Separate the whites from the yolks and place them in different bowls. Add to the yolks the sugar, flour and chocolate. Stir for five minutes. Whisk the egg whites until stiff and firm. Fold into yolk mixture until it forms a smooth and light substance.

Butter a round cake tin, put in the mixture and bake in a moderate oven for 15-20 minutes. Pin a white napkin round the tin, strew sifted sugar over the top of the soufflé and send it immediately to the table. If allowed to stand after it comes out of the oven, it will fall almost immediately.

Chocolate Truffles – makes about 44 truffles
Ingredients: 8 oz. semi-sweet or bittersweet chocolate chopped, 2/3 cup heavy cream, 2 Tbsp. cold butter. Coating: 8 oz. semi-sweet or bittersweet chocolate chopped, ½ cup unsweetened cocoa powder.

Mode: Place chocolate in bowl. In small saucepan heat cream with butter just until butter melts and bubbles around edge of pan; pour into chocolate whisking until smooth. Cover and refrigerate for two hours or until thickened and cold. Using melon baller or small spoon, scoop rounded teaspoonfuls dropping each onto waxed paper-lined tray. Press scraps together firmly, refrigerate for 30 minutes, and then continue scooping until all scraps are used. Gently roll each ball between fingertips to round off completely. Freeze for about one hour or until hard and almost frozen. Coating: In bowl over saucepan of hot (not boiling water), melt chocolate, stirring occasionally. Let cool slightly. Sift cocoa into pie plate. Using two forks, dip each ball into chocolate, letting excess drip off. (If chocolate thickens, rewarm gently.) Place balls in cocoa. Using two clean forks, roll truffles in cocoa; refrigerate on waxed paper-lined baking sheet until hardened. Place truffles in candy cups and refrigerate in airtight container for up to one week or frozen for up to three months. Variations: Orange truffles – reduce cream to ½ cup; add 3 Tbsp. orange liqueur to melted chocolate filling. Raspberry Truffles - Reduce cream to 1/3 cup. Press 1 cup fresh or thawed raspberries through fine sieve to remove seed and make ½ cup puree; add to chocolate filling.

"THE DINING-ROOM WAS A PLACE OF SHADOW AND GLOOM."

The Turkish bath

"Holmes and I had a weakness for the Turkish bath. It was over a smoke in the pleasant lassitude of the drying room that I have found him less reticent and more human than anywhere else. On the upper floor of the Northumberland Avenue establishment there is an isolated corner where two couches lie side by side, and it was on these that we lay upon September 3, 1902, the day when my narrative begins."

– Dr. John H. Watson in "The Illustrious Client"

Turkish Baths were popular from the moment they were introduced to the British Isles. Leslie Klinger writes in *The New Annotated Sherlock Holmes* that they were "…introduced to London Society by David Urquhart, a diplomat who served at the British Embassy in Turkey from 1831-1837." In the ensuing years of the 19th century, over 600 establishments opened in Britain, with 100 located in London. Some were attached to existing municipal bathing facilities, so the middle classes were not excluded from the benefits of the Turkish bath. This was an important factor since many homes at the time did not have bathing facilities.

The baths were regarded as "health spas" and were believed to have a positive effect on total physical well-being. As Dr. Watson noted in "The Disappearance of Lady Frances Carfax:" "But why Turkish?" asked Mr. Sherlock Holmes…. "Because for the last few days I have been feeling rheumatic and old. A Turkish bath is what we call an alterative in medicine – a fresh starting-point, a cleanser of the system."

The Turkish bath commences with relaxation in a room (known as the warm room) that is heated by a continuous flow of hot, dry air, allowing the bather to perspire freely. Bathers may then move to an even hotter room (known as the hot room) before they wash in cold water. After performing a full body wash and receiving a massage, bathers finally retire to the cooling room or drying room for a period of relaxation.

Some of the facilities were quite luxurious and boasted Royal Doulton basins, exotic tile work and even minarets on their architecture. The Turkish bath favoured by Holmes and Watson was "the Northumberland Avenue establishment known as the Charing Cross Baths or Nevills," according to Jack Tracy in his *Encyclopedia Sherlockiana*. There had been Turkish baths here since 1871 but the present building was opened by the Nevills in 1895. It is still possible to get some idea of the opulence of one of Nevill's nine London Turkish baths by visiting the restaurant which now occupies their former New Broad Street site.

Ladies enjoyed equally luxurious but separate facilities from the gentlemen, often at the same locations. I must say that the accommodations for ladies, albeit smaller than those for men, were lush and lovely.

Recipes

Easy Turkish Delight– Yield 1 and 3/4 pounds
Recipes for these delectable confections were brought back from Turkey by the crusaders. The 19th-century introduction of corn syrup and man-made gelatin made it possible for these candies to be made cheaply. Early references to them in English were called "lumps of delight." Nineteenth-century English jelly candies (of all sorts) were called Turkish Delights, beginning in 1877.

Ingredients: 3 envelopes unflavored gelatin, 2 cups sugar, 1/8 tsp. salt, 1 cup water (add some rose water to taste to make up cup), 1Tbsp. lemon or 1 tsp. orange juice, 1 tsp. lemon or 1tsp. orange rind – grated, red food coloring, powdered sugar.

Mode: Mix gelatin, sugar and salt in a heavy pot. Add water. Bring to slow boil and simmer without stirring for 10 minutes. Remove from heat and stir in juice and rind. Add a few drops of food colouring to turn the mixture a light pink. Taste for flavour; you may desire to add a bit more juice. Pour into 8-inch square pan which has been rinsed in cold water but not dried. Chill overnight. Cut into squares and roll each in powdered sugar.

Patlicanezmesi– Turkish smoked eggplant with yoghurt. Serves 2-4
Ingredients: 2 large eggplants, 3 cloves of garlic crushed with salt, juice of ½ a lemon, 1 Tbsp. olive oil, 2 Tbsp. good quality Balkan or Greek-style yoghurt, salt and freshly ground pepper. Fresh bread for dipping (pita or baguette).

Mode: Place the eggplants directly over a charcoal grill or gas flame, using the stems to turn them from time to time. The grilled eggplants are ready when they become soft and squishy, sometimes oozing a bit of juice. If you are using a gas flame, they are ready when the skin becomes burnt and flakey. Move the eggplants to a wooden board, and slit them open lengthwise using a sharp knife. Carefully scoop out the hot flesh, removing any flocks of burnt skin, and put the flesh into a bowl. Use a fork to mix in the olive oil, lemon juice and garlic and bind with yoghurt. Season to taste with salt and pepper and serve while still warm with bread.

The Criterion Bar and The Holborn Restaurant

"I was standing at the Criterion Bar, when someone tapped me on the shoulder, and turning around I recognized young Stamford "by Jove!" I cried; if he really wants someone to share the rooms and the expense, I am the very man for him." "You don't know Sherlock Holmes yet," he said; "perhaps you would not care for him as a constant companion." "In the exuberance of my joy, I asked him (Stamford) to have lunch with me at the Holborn, and we started off together in a hansom."

– Dr. John H. Watson & Stamford – A Study in Scarlet

I find it surprising that the young Dr. Watson, who was seeking a less expensive living arrangement, and professes that "so alarming did the state of my finances become…that I must make an alteration in my style of living" should be frequenting The Criterion Bar and The Holborn Restaurant. They are both of the highest quality and very dear in price.

Nonetheless, his choices proved to be most fortuitous. Jack Tracy, who wrote an excellent encyclopedia about my lodgers, describes The Criterion as a "…sumptuous restaurant, bar, and variety theatre, located in Regent Circus, Piccadilly. The bar is on the American pattern and is referred to as The Long Bar or the American Bar."

In 1870 a firm of wine merchants and caterers held a limited architectural competition to design a large restaurant, tavern and public rooms. The competition was won by architect Thomas Verity, and is regarded to be his best work. Building began in the summer of 1871 and was completed in 1873 at a cost of approximately £8,000,000 in today's currency. It is a splendid place with a Neo-Byzantine interior decorated in gold and marble. The Criterion is a five-level complex with the Long Bar located on the ground floor. The bar has a ceiling of gold mosaic, covered at the sides, and is decorated with a blue and white mosaic pattern. From its inception the new venture proved to be very profitable.

The restaurant soon gained a well-deserved reputation for serving fine modern British and European food. Its clientele included many royal and noble names, including Watson's literary agent, Arthur Conan Doyle. The restaurant was also a popular meeting place for women who were members of the suffrage movement and The Actresses Franchise League. The bar installed a plaque in 1953 to commemorate the historic meeting between Watson and Stamford. The Criterion is still listed by some as one of the top 10 most historic restaurants in the world, although it is now known as The Savini at Criterion. The plaque remains in place.

The Holborn Restaurant was located at 218 High Holborn, an area closely associated with the legal profession. In fact, there was a separate Lincoln's Inn entrance to accommodate the barristers. The Holborn was very popular with clubs and societies, including the Masons, who had their own hall above the restaurant. Novelist and historian Sir Walter Besant (1836-1901) stated that "it is a very gorgeous building and a palace of modern luxury." The Holborn survived until 1954, at which point it was converted into offices. Its iconic architecture, however, remains almost untouched.

The recipe I have chosen from The Holborn menu is a dish that the good doctor may have enjoyed. It dates back to the time of Chaucer.

Recipe

Salmis de Gibier– game birds or duck with mushrooms
Ingredients: 2 game birds roasted rare, 3 chopped shallots, 2 oz. butter,1 heaping Tbsp. flour, bouquet garni, thinly cut orange zest, pepper, salt, lemon juice, ¼ cup red or white wine, ¼ lb. sautéed mushrooms, large bread croûtons sautéed in butter, orange quarters.

Mode: Remove meat in nice, neat pieces from carcass. Use bones and trimmings to make 1 ½ cups of stock. Melt butter and cook shallots until rich, golden brown, then stir in flour and moisten with stock. Simmer 20 minutes with the bouquet garni, and orange zest and a bit of lemon juice until mixture is a rich, concentrated sauce – almost of a spoon-coating consistency. Strain into clean pan. Season to taste and add wine and mushrooms. Simmer five minutes, then add game, cover and leave for 10 minutes. The sauce should never boil once the game is added – it should barely simmer. Place pieces of game on top of the croûtons and serve sauce separately, or put the game and sauce into a serving dish, with croûtons tucked around edge. Garnish with orange quarters.

84

Country inns

"I have unwittingly condemned you to the horrors of a country inn."

– Sherlock Holmes in "The Retired Colourman"

Not all of the inns that Mr. Holmes and Dr. Watson visited were actually "horrors." Indeed, The Chequers Inn from "The Creeping Man" appears to have been frequented before by Mr. Holmes as he observed, "...the port was above mediocrity, and the linen beyond reproach." In total, the gentlemen frequented no less than seven inns in their published stories, including: The Westfield Arms from *Valley of Fear*, The Fighting Cock in the "Priory School," The Crown Inn from the "Speckled Band," The Green Dragon in "Shoscombe Old Place," The Black Swan from "The Copper Beeches," The Chequers (as mentioned above) and The Hereford Arms in "The Boscombe Valley Mystery."

The first inns were likely established when the Romans built their system of roads two millennia ago. Using archeological data, some inns can be traced as far back as 460 AD. The Domesday Book identifies one inn, being onsite in Stratfordshire since 1086. Inns tended to be older and grand establishments providing not only food and more extensive lodging than pubs but also stabling and fodder for traveller's horses and even fresh horses, should they be needed. Some of the earliest great inns were built by monasteries in centres of pilgrimage. Inns also served military purposes, with one of the oldest said to have been a recruiting station for volunteers to accompany King Richard I on his Crusade to the Holy Lands. In common with other tradesmen of the 14th century, inns began to display pictorial signs, which could be identified in an illiterate age. The earliest signs were drawn from heraldry but by Georgian times there were greater variations.

By 1577 it is estimated that there were some 2,000 inns throughout England and Wales. The larger inns had more scope for events. The type built with galleries around the courtyard provided an arena for plays and cockfights.

The inns played a large role in the 19th century with the expansion of the English railway transportation system. Industry was on the rise and people were travelling more to keep and maintain business. The inn was an important part of English infrastructure as they helped maintain a smooth flow of travel throughout the country.

Inns, like pubs, also acted as community gathering places. Indeed, Mr. Holmes believed that here were the best places to collect local gossip as he observed in "The Adventure of the Solitary Cyclist."

The Hereford Arms in "The Boscombe Valley Mystery" was in the Midlands, an area known as the home for Melton Mowbray pork pies and the happy accident of two chemists, Lea and Perrins, who were working on developing a new spiced condiment for one of their customers. The original batch was too strong and was left in a barrel in the basement of their shop only to be rediscovered some time later when it fermented and mellowed. The partners then sold it with great success. The region is also the home of Stilton and Cheshire cheeses, the latter being made continuously from the 12th century. Notable, too, is the cider, which has a much higher alcohol content than usual.

Many romantic legends grew around inns. Tales of ghosts, highwaymen, royal connections and tunnels are but just a few elements in the mythology. Mr. Holmes would no doubt caution us to believe nothing unless it can be substantiated from primary sources.

Recipes

Lamb Chops with Mustard Sauce – serves 4
Ingredients: 1 Tbsp. rosemary leaves finely chopped, 4 Tbsp. olive oil, 8 loin lamb chops, scant ½ cup lamb or beef stock, 2 Tbsp. wholegrain Dijon mustard, 1 tsp. Worcestershire sauce, salt and ground black pepper, 2/3 cup sour cream.

Mode: Mix rosemary with olive oil and rub mixture over chops. Let stand 30 minutes or longer if chilled. Season lightly with salt and pepper. Heat a large frying pan, add the chops and cook over medium heat for 5-8 minutes per side until cooked. Lift chops out of pan and keep warm. Pour the stock into the hot pan, scraping up any sediment and add the mustard and sour cream. Bubble gently for 2-3 minutes. Heat until mixture comes to a boil and is reduced by about ⅓. Stir in Worcestershire sauce and adjust seasoning. Serve chops with mustard sauce spooned over.

Jugged Hare (or Rabbit) – serves 6
Ingredients: 1 hare jointed, salt, pepper, mace, bouquet garni, 1 onion stuck with 3 cloves, ¼ lb. butter, ½ cup red or white wine, 1 anchovy chopped, pinch Cayenne pepper, 1 Tbsp. butter, 1 Tbsp. flour, triangles of fried bread. Lemon juice if desired.

Mode: Put the pieces in a large stoneware jug after rubbing them with salt, pepper and mace. Add the bouquet, onion and butter. Cover the jug tightly and securely with foil and string to make sure it keeps its place. Stand the jug in a pan of boiling water and keep it simmering until the hare is cooked – about 3 hours, but the time depends on the age and toughness of the creature. This can be done on top of the stove or in the oven if more convenient. Removed the cooked pieces to a serving dish. Strain the juices into a pan. Add the wine, anchovy and pepper to taste. Thicken with the flour and butter mashed together and add in little knobs. The sauce must not boil again once the wine has been added or it will curdle. Season with a little lemon juice if desired.

"WITH DIFFICULTY HE LIMPED UP TO THE DOOR."

Sherlock Holmes and Dr. Watson arrive at The Fighting Cock Inn during "The Adventure of the Priory School"

Beekeeping in Sussex

"There are certain pursuits which, if not wholly poetic and true, do at least suggest a nobler and finer relation to nature than we know. The keeping of bees, for instance."

— Henry David Thoreau

Dear Mr. Holmes was only 49 when he retired to Sussex to keep bees. His relentless, self-sacrificing pursuit of criminals and justice had taken its toll on his constitution after 23 years of active practice, with 17 of those years spent in partnership with Dr. Watson. He purchased a little farm in Sussex Downs, a lovely southern county of England, five miles from Eastbourne. His home, which I visited several times, had beautiful views overlooking the English Channel. He described the coast line as "entirely of chalk cliffs which can only be descended by a single, long tortuous path, which is steep and slippery."

The location was set back, Mr. Holmes explained, because one cannot keep bees on a cliff edge. He was very familiar with Sussex, as many of his documented cases either mentioned it or occurred there. Mr. Holmes engaged an elderly woman, Martha, from the village to serve as his housekeeper. Some individuals assume this person to be myself but I was his landlady and not a housekeeper per se. I did some special duties for both the good doctor and Mr. Holmes but never the daily chores expected of a housekeeper. Martha saw to Mr. Holmes's needs admirably, even providing professional assistance once, as I had occasion to do in London.

When Mr. Holmes was not engaged in special assignments during The Great War, he devoted himself to readings of a philosophical nature, as well as becoming an expert in the applied science of beekeeping. He wrote a highly regarded book, titled *Practical Handbook of Bee Culture, with Some Observations upon the Segregation of the Queen*. As he told Dr. Watson, "Behold the fruit of pensive nights and laborious days when I watched the little working gangs as once I watched the criminal world of London."

Here are a few fascinating facts about beekeeping that I learned from Mr. Holmes:

Approximately one-third of all food eaten is directly or indirectly derived from honeybee pollination. Some crops that are pollinated are: almonds, carrot seed, melons, apricots, cherries, pears, apples, plums, onions and blueberries. On average, a worker bee lasts six to eight weeks in the summer. Their most common cause of death is wearing out their wings. During that six- to eight-week period, their average honey production is 1/12 of a teaspoon. In such a brief lifetime, they fly the equivalent of 1 1/2 times the circumference of the Earth. Beekeeping dates back at least 4,500 years.

Queen Elizabeth II employs a 'Royal Beekeeper' in the Buckingham Palace gardens. One of her special gifts to visiting dignitaries is a jar of this very singular honey.

Recipes

Roast Parsnips with Honey and Nutmeg: (Parsnips were introduced in England by the Romans in 55 BC) – Serves 4-6

Ingredients: 4 medium parsnips peeled and cut lengthwise into quarters, 2 Tbsp. all-purpose flour seasoned with salt and pepper, 4 Tbsp. oil, 2 Tbsp. honey, grated nutmeg.

Mode: Preheat oven to 400F. Cook parsnips in pan of boiling water, cook for 5 minutes until slightly soft. Drain thoroughly then dredge in flour; shake off excess. Add oil to roasting pan and place in oven until hot. Add parsnips, tossing in oil and arrange in single layer. Return pan to oven and cook 30 minutes turning occasionally until crisp, golden and cooked through. Drizzle with honey and a little grated nutmeg. Return to oven for 5 minutes before serving.

Honey Cake– Makes 2 loaves

Ingredients: 1¼ cups sugar, ¾ cup Earl Grey tea at room temperature, ½ cup canola oil, 1 cup honey, 2 large eggs at room temperature, 2½ cups all-purpose flour, 2½ tsp. baking powder, pinch black pepper, pinch grated nutmeg, 1 heaping teaspoon cinnamon, 1 tsp. ground ginger, 1 cup walnut halves.

Mode: Preheat oven to 350F. Take two loaf pans, each measuring 9x5½x3¼ inches, and grease and flour them. Mix together all ingredients except for walnuts and blend well. Stir in walnuts. Pour batter into prepared pans and bake 35 to 40 minutes, or until a cake tester inserted in the centre comes clean. Cool and remove from pans. Slice thin and serve with butter at breakfast or with tea. If covered with foil they will keep two weeks and improve with time.

Mead – Introduced by the Anglo-Saxons in the 5th century following the fall of the Roman Empire)
Ingredients: 2½ Tbsp. hops, ⅔ cup honey, 5 cups water, slice of lemon.

Mode: Place hops in muslin/cheesecloth bag. Put all ingredients in a large saucepan and bring to boil. Simmer 30 minutes. Remove scum from time to time. Cool and strain through muslin into large glass jar or stone crock. Do not fill more than ¾ full to allow fermentation. Cover with muslin and leave until fermentation stops, about three weeks. Pour into bottles and cork, or leave in the jar, also corked. Label and store in a cool, dark place.

Currying flavour

"The regiment was stationed in India at the time…"

– *Dr. John H. Watson in* A Study in Scarlet

As described in A Study in Scarlet, after training as a military surgeon at Netly Military Hospital, dear Dr. Watson was attached to the Fifth Northumberland Fusiliers and was briefly stationed in Bombay. The Fusiliers joined forces with the 66th (Berkshire) Regiment of Foot under the command of Brigadier George Burrows. They engaged the forces of Afghanistan leader Ayyub Kahn at Maiwand on 27 July, 1880. The objective was part of a British campaign to stop Russian influence in Afghanistan, as this threatened British control in India. I read in the newspapers of the time that the strength of the forces are generally held to be only 2,500 British and Indian troops facing 3,000 Afghan cavalry and 9,000 infantry. What ensued was deemed to be one of the bloodiest battles of the three Anglo-Afghan wars (1839-42, 1878-80, 1919). It was during this horrific campaign that Dr. Watson was severely wounded by a Jezail bullet. The Afghan snipers were notoriously accurate and the .50 -.70 calibre bullets were filled with everything from iron nails to pebbles and thus were particularly deadly. It was only through the efforts of his orderly, Murray, that Dr. Watson survived the main wound to his shoulder. His wound from such a high-calibre rifle could have done more damage to his body, especially if he were bent over, as some have postulated, which may explain his troublesome leg. He was sent to Peshawar in India (now part of Pakistan) to recover. It was during his time in India that Dr. Watson developed an affinity for curries and other Indian dishes. In fact, Queen Victoria, Empress of India, was noted to be so fond of curries that she had Indian staff prepare them every day.

The first Indian spices were present in English cookery since the time of the Crusades in the late 11th century. According to the Muslim Museum Initiative, "the first appearance of curry on a menu was at The Norris Street Coffee House in Haymarket, London in 1773. By 1784 curry and rice had become house specialties in some fashionable restaurants in London's Piccadilly." An ingenious Bengali immigrant, Sake Dean Mahomed, a captain of the East India Company, a surgeon and the first Indian to publish books in English, is said to have founded London's first Indian restaurant – The Hindoostane Coffee House in 1810. It was located originally at 34 George Street – now renumbered to 102 between Gloucester Place and Baker Street. It was awarded a historical plaque by the City of Westminster in 2005.

Hannah Glasse's The Art of Cookery Made Plain and Simple, published in 1747, is one of the first cookbooks to give recipes for curries and pulaos (rice dishes). However, it was not until the British Raj began in 1858 that returning Britons clamoured for the tastes of the cuisine that they enjoyed in India. Many dishes were adapted in Anglo-Indian recipes such as kedgeree and mulligatawny soup. By the end of the 19th century there were approximately 70,000 South Asians living in Britain.

The late foreign secretary, Robin Cook, declared the derivative Anglo-Indian curry chicken tikka masala as Britain's national dish in 2001. There are currently over 10,000 curry houses in the U.K., employing over 80,000 staff and serving around 2.5 million customers every week.

Dr. Watson and Mr. Holmes shared a distinct penchant for new or exotic cuisines. Dr. Watson certainly relished the idea of introducing Mr. Holmes to his passion for Indian food whilst Mr. Holmes invited Dr. Watson to dine with him at Goldini's Italian restaurant at the end of The Bruce Partington Plans.

Recipes

Mrs. Beeton's 1861 Recipe for Curry-powder
She also provides recipes for Indian Mustard, Indian Pickle, and Indian Chetney [sic.] Sauce.

Ingredients: ¼ lb. coriander seed, ¼ lb. turmeric, 2 oz. cinnamon seed, ½ oz. cayenne, 1 oz. mustard, 1oz. ground ginger, ½ oz. allspice, 2 oz. fenugeek seed.

Mode: Put all ingredients in a cool oven, where they should remain one night; then pound them in a mortar, rub them through a sieve, and mix thoroughly together. Keep the powder in a bottle from which air is completely excluded.

Mrs. Beeton notes that*: "we have given this recipe for curry-powder, as some persons prefer to make it at home; but that purchased at any respectable shop is, generally speaking far superior, and taking all things into consideration, very frequently more economical. "*

Mango Chutney – An Anglo-Indian Dish. Makes 1 cup. May store in fridge up to 1 week.
Ingredients: ¼ cup brown sugar, ⅓ cup raisins, ¼ tsp. freshly ground nutmeg, pinch of salt, 2 cups mango coarsely chopped, 2 Tbsp. lime juice, ¼ cup white vinegar, 4 whole cloves, ½ tsp. cinnamon, 1 small onion finely chopped, 2 Tbsp. water, ½ small chopped chili (optional).

Mode: In non-reactive pan, combine sugar, vinegar, raisins, cloves, nutmeg, cinnamon, salt and onions. Bring mixture to a boil, then reduce to slow simmer and cook for 10 minutes. Add mango and water then simmer until thick, stirring often. Remove from heat and stir in lime juice. Serve at room temperature as a cooling agent for spicy dishes.

Pork Vindaloo – Serves 6-8. Adjust oven rack to lower 1/3 position and preheat oven to 300F.

Ingredients: 3 lbs. pork stew meat cut into 1 ¼ inch cubes, salt and pepper, 3 Tbsp. oil or ghee (Indian clarified butter), 8 cloves of garlic, minced, 3 medium onions coarsely chopped, 3 Tbsp. flour, 1 Tbsp. paprika, ¾ tsp. ground cumin, ½ tsp. ground cardamom, ¼ tsp. cayenne pepper, ¼ tsp. ground cloves, 1 tsp. sugar, 1 ½ cups chicken broth, 14.5 oz. tin diced tomatoes, 2 bay leaves, 2 Tbsp. red wine vinegar, 1 Tbsp. mustard seeds, ½ cup minced parsley leaves.

Mode: Dry meat with paper towels and season generously with salt and pepper. Heat 1 Tbsp. of oil or ghee in a Dutch oven over medium heat until it shimmers. Add ½ of the meat and cook not moving until well browned. Turn and brown all sides of meat until browned, about five minutes longer. Transfer pork and juices to medium bowl. Repeat with other ½ of the meat. Reduce heat to medium and add remaining 1 Tbsp. of oil to pot and coat bottom. Add onions, ¼ tsp. salt and cook vigourously, scraping bottom and edges until onions have softened, about 5 minutes. Stir in garlic and cook 30 minutes. Add flour, paprika, cumin, cardamom, cayenne and cloves. Stir until onions are evenly coated and fragrant, about two minutes. Gradually add broth, tomatoes, bay leaves, sugar, vinegar, mustard seeds and bring to simmer. Add pork and juices. Return to simmer, cover and place in oven. Cook two hours. Remove from oven. Skim off any fat, remove bay leaves, stir in parsley and adjust seasonings. Serve immediately with basmati rice.

Quick Basmati Rice Variations –Serves 2- 4
Ingredients: 1 cup basmati rice, 1 ½ cups of water. Cook as directed.

Mode: **Pulao** – 2 tsp. ghee (Indian clarified butter) or peanut oil, 2 tsp. coconut ground to a powder, 2 tsp. ground almonds, 1 tsp. fennel seeds, 1 tsp black cumin seeds. Heat ghee and stir fry spices for 30 seconds. Add other ingredients and stir into rice until hot. **Lemon Rice** – 2 tsp. ghee or peanut oil, 2 Tbsp. toasted cashews, 1 tsp. coconut ground to a powder, juice of 2 lemons, 1 tsp. mustard seeds, 1 tsp. sesame seeds, 1 tsp turmeric, 6 fresh or dry curry leaves. Heat ghee or oil and stir fry spices for 30 seconds. Add other ingredients and stir well into rice until hot. **Saffron Rice** – Soak a few threads of saffron in 3 Tbsp. water for 30 minutes. Pour over rice and return lid to pot for 5 minutes so aroma does not escape. Stir well before serving hot.

Lamb Kabobs – Maybe barbequed or broiled on skewers. Chopped meat can also be added to a salad. Accompany with naan. Serves 4.

Ingredients: 1 lb. ground lamb, 1 medium onion finely chopped, 2 Tbsp. plain good-quality Balkan or Greek-style yoghurt, ½ tsp. crushed garlic, 1 tsp. ground coriander, 1 tsp. chili powder, 3 Tbsp. garam masala, finely chopped fresh parsley, 2 green chilies finely chopped (optional), ½ tsp. finely grated ginger, 1 tsp. ground cumin, ½ tsp. salt, ½ tsp. ground allspice, ¼ tsp. ground cardamom, small pinch ground cloves, ½ tsp. ground black pepper, 1 tsp. dried mint, 2 Tbsp. melted ghee or oil, 1 Tbsp. vinegar, 1 lime cut in wedges for garnish.

Mode: Mix onions, parsley, mint and chilies (if using) in a bowl. In separate bowl, mix yoghurt with ginger, garlic, cumin, coriander, salt, black pepper, chili powder, allspice, garam masala, cardamom, cloves. Blend with onion mixture. Blend the combined mixture into ground lamb and mix well with hands. Divide into eight equal portions. Using wet hands, shape the mixture into balls. Thread three onto each skewer. Brush kebabs with melted ghee or oil and broil or barbeque until cooked through and well browned on the surface. Serve immediately with lime wedges and raita.

Raita – Serves 4-6 as accompaniment to hot or spicy dishes.

Ingredients: 1 large cucumber, 1 ½ tsp. salt, ½ cup plain good quality Greek or Balkan-style yoghurt, 3 tsp. chopped fresh mint.

Mode: Peel cucumber, cut in half and scoop out seeds with a teaspoon. Coarsely grate the cucumber into a bowl, sprinkle with salt, and let sit 5-6 minutes. Drain off accumulated liquid. Stir yoghurt and mint into cucumber. Serve in small dishes. Alternatively, the cucumber may also be peeled, thinly sliced and salted to extract juices and folded through the yoghurt.

Some background on Mrs. Hudson

My older brother, Robert, had rooms at the Albany, an exclusive address for men of means. There he met Mr. Alec Hudson (a fellow Scot) and they became close friends. Alec had impeccable qualifications as an architect and was in demand for public and private commissions.

Robert invited Alec to dinner at our home. I was smitten by him. He was handsome, intelligent and had a delightful sense of humour. We were wed just six months later. Alec purchased 221 Baker Street as our home and his office whilst he built us a house of his own design.

Shortly thereafter, Alec met two gentlemen for a brief meeting on a lucrative project being led by Stephan T. Ward and Lord Jonathan Chase. The financial terms were one-third upon signing the contract, one-third when building commenced and final payment upon completion.

Lord Jonathan did not remit the first payment on time, citing late receipt of capital from a silent partner. Alec also learned that the workmen on the site were not being paid for their labours. The project began in great financial uncertainty.

Alec arranged a meeting at his club with Lord Jonathan and Mr. Ward at his club. A most heated discussion ensued. Alec withdrew all association with the project. He intended to report the nefarious goings-on to the Royal Institute of British Architects and the police because he suspected that the men had been involved with fraud on other projects he heard about as well.

Several nights later, Alec visited his club on Friday, as was his wont. At 3 a.m. I heard loud knocks on the front door. A police constable and a plainclothes detective from Scotland Yard said they believed Mr. Alec Hudson was a victim of foul play. They required me to accompany them to headquarters. I asked the constable to call upon my brother to meet us at our destination.

We were taken to the morgue. Alec had been stabbed in the back. The detective handed me his gold cuff links, stickpin, watch and chain, and billfold containing £100. I inquired about possible suspects and was told that it looked to be the work of a common footpad interrupted before he could take his plunder. I explained Alec's recent confrontation and allegations against the developer and the builder. The detective, Mr. Lestrade, stated that since there were no eyewitnesses to the murder, it was unlikely a case could ever be proven. Without tangible evidence, he could not approach men the calibre of Lord Jonathan or Mr. Ward. I was devastated.

Five years later, Sherlock Holmes came into my life. He was keen to rent the first floor of 221 Baker Street. I inquired about his professional references. When he stated that he was the world's first and only private consulting detective, I was intrigued. I shared Alec's story with him. He regarded Inspector Lestrade as the best of a bad lot. The Detective Branch had been reorganized and was now known as the Criminal Investigating Department (CID). Mr. Holmes applied his methods and examined the facts of the case and conducted an exhaustive investigation. Sadly, he reported that the possible suspects had disappeared and that the trail had gone cold. I chose never to remarry. I could never hope to find another I would love as much as Alec Hudson.

Recipes

Haggis– Serves 4-6. Serve with neeps (mashed swede or turnip) and tatties (mashed potatoes).

Ingredients: 1 sheep's stomach or ox secum, cleaned and thoroughly scalded, turned inside out and soaked overnight in cold salted water; cleaned heart and lungs, and liver (optional) of 1 lamb; 1lb. beef or lamb trimmings, fat and lean; 2 onions, finely chopped; 8 oz. oatmeal; 1 Tbsp. salt; 1 tsp. ground black pepper; 1 tsp. ground dried coriander; 1 tsp. mace; 1 tsp. nutmeg; water, enough to cook the haggis; stock from lungs and trimmings.

Mode: Wash the lungs, heart and liver (if using). Place in large pan of cold water with the meat trimmings and bring to the boil. Cook for about two hours. When cooked, strain off the stock and set the stock aside. Mince the lungs, heart, liver and trimmings. Put the minced mixture in a bowl and add the finely chopped onions, oatmeal and seasoning. Mix well and add enough stock to moisten the mixture. It should have a soft crumbly consistency. Spoon the mixture into the sheep's stomach, so it's just over half full. Sew up the stomach with strong white cotton thread and prick a couple of times so it doesn't explode while cooking. Put the haggis in a pan of boiling water (enough to cover it) and cook for three hours without a lid. Keep adding more water to keep it covered. To serve, cut open the haggis and spoon out the filling. Serves 4-6 with neeps (mashed swede or turnip) and tatties (mashed potatoes).

Traditional Scottish Shortbread

Ingredients: 1 cup butter, 1 cup sugar, 3½ cups all-purpose flour.

Mode: Cream butter and sugar. Add 3½ cups flour, ½ cup at a time. Mix well and knead thoroughly. Add more flour if needed.

The more you knead, the tastier the shortbread will be. Pat the dough into a round, baking tin (don't roll it or grease the pan; the dough is rich enough). Prick with a fork all the way through, top to bottom, in a design if you can. Cut slightly into wedge sections. Bake in 300F (very slow) oven for 45-60 minutes. Do not let shortbread get brown on top.

Finnan Haddie– Serves 2-4

Ingredients: 1 lb. smoked haddock; 1 large onion, thinly sliced, 14 oz. of milk, ½ tsp. cracked pepper; 1½ tsp. mustard powder, 1 oz. butter, softened, 2 tsp. all-purpose flour; 1 finely chopped spring onion; some finely chopped parsley for garnish.

Mode: Place the thinly sliced onion in the base of a large pan. Cut the smoked haddock into pieces about ½ to an inch wide and spread over the onion. Mix the milk, pepper and mustard and pour over the fish. Bring to a boil slowly, reduce the heat to low and simmer covered for five minutes. Then uncover and simmer for another five minutes. Remove the fish from the pan with a slotted spoon to allow the juices to run off and place in a warm serving dish. Continue to simmer the mixture in the pan for another five minutes, stirring frequently.

Mix the softened butter and flour, and add to the pan along with the finely chopped spring onion. Stir over a low heat until the mixture comes to a slow boil and thickens slightly. Pour over the fish and garnish with some finely chopped parsley.

Menu

Ox-tail Soup.

Turbot,
Ravigote Sauce.

Mutton Cutlets and
Spinach.

Roast Goose,
Apple Sauce.
Potatoes. Savoys.

Salad.

Cabinet Pudding.
Lemon Jelly.

Menu

Clear Soup.

Cod Steaks,
Tartar Sauce.

Rissolettes of Game.

Sirloin of Beef,
Horseradish Sauce.
Potatoes. Sprouts.

Wild Duck.

Olives.

Apple Tart and
Cream.
Stone Cream.

Menu

Mock Turtle Soup.

Brill,
Oyster Sauce.

Beef Olives.
Stuffed Tomatoes

Roast Leg of Mutton.
Potatoes.
Mashed Turnips.

Black Game.

Charlotte Russe.
Compôte of Peaches.

Menu

Oyster Soup.

Red Mullet.

Hashed Game.

Stewed Fillet of Beef,
Piquante Sauce.
Mashed Potatoes.

Snipe.

Chocolate Soufflé.
Marbled Jelly.

Cheese Straws.

Illness, medicine, poison and Mrs. Hudson

"...a telegram from Lyons which informed me that Holmes was lying ill... Within 24 hours I was in his sickroom...even his iron constitution, however, had broken down under the strain of an investigation."

– Dr. John H. Watson in "The Reigate Squire"

"Drink this. I dashed some brandy into the water, and the colour began to come back to his bloodless checks...I sponged the wound, cleaned it, dressed it and finally covered it over with cotton wadding and carbolized bandages."

– Dr. John H. Watson in "The Engineer's Thumb"

We were very fortunate to live during a time of great advances in medicine. Nitrous oxide was first used. The stethoscope and thermometer were invented. Carbolic acid was employed as a disinfectant. Additionally, *The Lancet* was first published (Dr. Watson is an avid reader of this publication), the use of chloroform for surgery was developed, and germ theory led to diagnoses for scarlet fever, croup, syphilis, gonorrhea, typhoid and typhus.

Great advances were made but great threats remained. It was not until 1850 that it was recognized that both cholera and typhoid were transmitted through drinking water that was contaminated with faeces. Legislation to improve London's water supply was passed in 1855. In 1872 the Food, Drink and Drugs Act protected the poor by eliminating adulterated foods such as plaster of Paris in bread, rotten over-spiced food and strychnine in beer. Fog caused respiratory diseases that led to pneumonia and pleurisy, resulting in thousands of deaths. Tuberculosis accounted for more than 20 million deaths during the 19th century. Although the poor were most affected, Queen Victoria's beloved husband Prince Albert was among those who succumbed.

Physicians were exalted over surgeons for many years. Doctors attended medical school for three or four years or more, whereas surgeons merely apprenticed for a year. The surgeons were considered glorified butchers. The best of the lot were those who could amputate in the shortest length of time. Thus, they held the title of simply "Mr.", which continues to the present day.

Doctors were expensive and ministered predominantly to the middle and upper classes. A Harley Street address was highly desirable, as it is today. Medical school graduates could become Fellows of the Royal College of Physicians(FRCP). Dear Dr. Watson had to take special instruction in surgery before he went out to the war in Afghanistan and thus is very qualified both as a physician and surgeon. Most doctors perceived their role simply as observing the patient's symptoms, deciding upon a diagnosis, and prescribing medications and diet. Hands-on ministering such as palpating, and use of the recently-invented stethoscope were avoided until other physicians had success with these new methods.

The poor could not afford the luxury of doctors. They relied on apothecaries, chemists and druggists. In dire straits, the poor resorted to overcrowded and filthy hospitals. The nurses were often inebriated and simply changed the slops and delivered watery gruel for meals. When Florence Nightingale returned from Scutari in the Crimea, she was horrified at the conditions and nursing staff. She founded the Nightingale School of Nursing at St. Thomas Hospital. The first students were admitted in 1860. Her graduates were considered to be "true professional women." Miss Nightingale had more medical skills than many Harley Street physicians. In 1907 she became the first woman to receive The Order of Merit. Miss Nightingale, ill and weak, worked well into her 90s.

The century also produced a plethora of so-called patent medicines (which did not have patents at all). Apothecaries, chemists, druggists and pharmacists enjoyed a surge in business from the poor and middle class, who sought cures for every ailment. Jesse Boots took over the family chemist shop in 1877. By 1931 there were more than 1,000 Boots the Chemist outlets in Great Britain. Druggists, chemists and pharmacists developed numerous remedies. These were often poisonous, habit forming or ineffective products. Their ingredients, included laudanum, opium, morphine, cocaine and arsenic. Many had high concentrations of alcohol, lead, zinc, mercury and digitalis.

Nourishing Meals for the Invalid (Approved by Florence Nightingale)

These are rules to be observed in cooking for invalids:

- Let all the kitchen utensils be delicately and scrupulously clean.
- Never make a large quantity of one thing and it is desirable that variety be provided for them.

- Always have something in readiness should the invalid desire sustenance. If obliged to wait too long, the patient loses his or her desire to eat.
- In sending food to the invalid, let everything look as tempting as possible.
- Have a clean tray cloth; let the spoons, tumblers, cups and saucers be very clean and bright. Gruel is more appetizing when served in a tumbler.
- As milk is an important food for the sick, in warm weather let it be kept on ice. Many other delicacies may be preserved in this manner for a little time. If the invalid is allowed to eat vegetables, never send them undercooked or raw. Let a small quantity be cut into small pieces and temptingly arranged on the pieces.
- Never leave food in a sickroom. If the patient cannot eat it, take it away and bring it back in an hour or two. Miss Nightingale says, "To leave the patient's food by his side, from meal to meal, in hope he will eat it in the interval, is simply to prevent him from taking food at all."

Revolutionary Products

Three inventions made caring for the ill much easier. Bovril was created in 1870 by John Lawson Johnston as a simpler beef tea. Alfred Bird was a qualified chemist, druggist and registered pharmacist. His wife was unable to digest eggs, bread or yeast but was very partial to custard. After six years of work, he formulated Bird's Custard Powder in 1837. There was a large demand for a way to improve the taste of meat that was not always fresh and a desire to enhance bland foods. Mr. Lea, a pharmacist from Worcester, and his assistant Mr. Perrins introduced Worcestershire sauce, to great acclaim. The formula was a closely held secret until it was uncovered in 1980.

As I reflect upon the sad and dangerous items about which I have just written, I thank heaven I have as lodgers dear Mr. Holmes, who is a superb chemist and knowledgeable about all manner of poisons, and Dr. Watson, who is an experienced modern physician and surgeon with his wits about him.

Recipes

Nutritious Coffee

Ingredients: ½ oz. ground coffee, 2 cups whole milk.

Mode: Put coffee into a saucepan, with the milk, which should be made nearly boiling before the coffee is put in, and boil both together for three minutes. Clear it by pouring some of it into a cup, and then back again, and leave it on the hob for a few minutes to settle thoroughly. This coffee is made still more nutritious by the addition of an egg, well beaten and put into the coffee cup.

Egg Wine

Ingredients: 1 egg, 1 Tbsp. and ½ glass cold water, 1 glass sherry, sugar and grated nutmeg to taste.

Mode: Beat the egg, mixing it with 1 Tbsp. of cold water. Make the wine and glass of water hot but not boiling; pour it on the egg, stirring all the time. Add sufficient lump sugar to sweeten the mixture, and a little grated nutmeg. Put all into a very clean saucepan, set it on a gentle fire and stir the contents one way until it thickens but do not allow them to boil. Serve in a glass with snippets of toasted bread or plain crisp biscuits. When the egg is not warmed, the mixture will be found easier of digestion but it is not so pleasant a drink.

MELLIN'S FOOD

For INFANTS and INVALIDS.

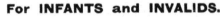

"*33, Alkham Road, Stoke Newington,*
"*5th March, 1894.*

"*Dear Sir,—I have great pleasure in inclosing a photograph of my little daughter, Vera Florence, taken when she was nine months old. For the first three months she was very delicate, and though nursing her myself, she suffered from acute indigestion, and could not retain her natural food. I was advised to wean her and give her your Food, and the result was that from taking the first bottle she showed great improvement. She has been brought up entirely on your Food ever since, and is a fine, healthy child, and at the time her photo. was taken had twelve teeth, four of them double, and could almost walk alone. I may add she is now twelve months old, and can walk well, and has fourteen teeth. I am naturally very pleased, and recommend your Food to all my friends.*
"*Yours truly,*
"*ALICE SIBLEY.*"

MELLIN'S FOOD BISCUITS

(Manufactured by Carr & Co., Carlisle, specially for G. Mellin).

DIGESTIVE.   NOURISHING.   SUSTAINING.

For Children after Weaning, the Aged, Dyspeptic, and for all who require a Simple Nutritious and Sustaining Food. Price 2/- and 3/6 per tin.

AN ILLUSTRATED PAMPHLET ON THE FEEDING AND REARING OF INFANTS.—A Practical and Simple Treatise for Mothers, containing a large number of Portraits of Healthy and Beautiful Children, together with Facsimiles of Original Testimonials, which are of the greatest interest to all mothers, to be had, with samples, free by post, on application.

MELLIN'S FOOD WORKS, STAFFORD STREET, PECKHAM, S.E.

110

Mrs. Hudson upon Victorian values towards women

"The modest virgin, the prudent wife, and the careful matron, are much more serviceable in life than petticoated philosophers, blustering heroines, or virago queens. She who makes her husband and her children happy, who reclaims the one from vice and trains up the other to virtue, is a much greater character than ladies described in romances, whose whole occupation is to murder mankind with shafts from their quiver, or their eyes."

– Oliver Goldsmith in *The Vicar of Wakefield*

In her *Book of Household Management*, Mrs. Beeton describes no less than 54 duties and virtues of "the mistress of the house" covering everything from "Early Rising," "Friendships," "Hospitality" and "The Important Subject of Dress and Fashion." Essentially, the upper and middle classes of a Victorian women's lives were dictated by societal expectations and restrictions. These values were exemplified by Queen Victoria who was a role model for familial closeness and duty. Only the advent of the Industrial Revolution brought about some changes for the women of lower classes, as they were needed to add to the workforce. However, their wages were lower than men's for the same work and they were expected to perform all the wifely chores and duties of maintaining a family and household as well. Women were the chattel of men – divorce for a woman was almost unattainable and if she did succeed she was cast out of society, never to see her children again. Women were perceived to be unable to comprehend the superior knowledge of men and were deemed the weaker sex in general. A woman's role was completely and utterly subordinate to man's.

I was extremely fortunate that my solicitor father regarded my formal education with the same importance he ascribed to that of my brother, Robert. In this more liberal household I was not treated as a "possession" to be handed over with all my worldly goods to any "suitable" husband. Indeed, my father ensured that I should have a prenuptial agreement guaranteeing my access to my own property of jewels, pin money and other worldly goods in an estate that I may possess for my sole and separate use not subject to the control of my husband. I am indeed thankful that I met and married Alec Hudson, who shared these values and respected the human rights of women. But despite this point of view and attempted safeguards for a legacy of my own, the Married Woman's Property act of 1870 nevertheless provided that all property in a woman's name before marriage still belonged to her husband after marriage. Once married, the only way that women could reclaim property was through widowhood. It was only through the tragedy of Alec's murder that I was able to – as provided in his will – maintain control over our property and my inheritance, and owned land since by law any unmarried adult female was considered to be a *"feme sole."* It wasn't until 1893 that the Third Woman's Property Act gave women control of their own property.

Thus, I came to inherit 221 Baker Street and became the landlady to Mr. Holmes and Dr. Watson. The rental of their rooms augmented my inheritance, which amounted to a healthy and steady annual income. My earlier education prepared me for the efficient running of a household and for that I thank my insightful father. Mr. Holmes and Dr. Watson took up their rooms in originally in 1881 but by 1889 Mr. Holmes paid me a rather "princely sum" as was reported in "The Adventure of the Dying Detective." This, of course was due to my increasing involvement with Mr. Holmes's consulting practice and the very real dangers it imposed.

I also became involved with the Women's Suffrage Movement, beginning in 1898 with the National Union of Women's Suffrage Societies (NUWSS) and changing to Mrs. Pankhurst's group, The Women's Social Political Union (WSPU), which was more politically radical. Coincidentally, the WSPU held its afternoon tea meetings at the Criterion Restaurant, the locale of Dr. Watson's meeting with Mr. Sanford that resulted in the good doctor's subsequent sharing of rooms with Mr. Sherlock Holmes at 221B. The Criterion was chosen by the WSPU due to its renowned afternoon teas. I am pleased that the Criterion of today still offers afternoon teas – albeit at exceptionally high prices: A Cream Tea of scones, with a selection of jams and clotted cream and biscuits is £ 16.25, Afternoon Tea with the above plus finger sandwiches and pastry is £ 29.25, and a glass of Champagne or Martini Afternoon Tea with the Cream Tea Menu is £ 39.25. Here are recipes for some of my favourites from earlier times at the Criterion.

Recipes

Victoria Sandwich– serves 8-10
Preheat oven to 350F, grease and line 2 - 8" cake pans,

Ingredients: ½ cup superfine sugar, ½ cup soft butter, 1 tsp. vanilla extract, 3 large eggs at room temperature, ½ cup self-rising flour, ¾ cup whole milk, 4-5 Tbsp. raspberry jam, ½ cup whipping (heavy) cream, confectioner's sugar (icing sugar) for dusting.

Mode: Beat the sugar, butter and vanilla extract until pale and light, then beat in the eggs a little at a time to make a mousse-like consistency. You can do this with an electric mixer. Fold in the flour by hand (don't beat it in or the cake may be tough). Add enough milk to make a dropping consistency. (Hold a spoon loaded with mixture sideways, and give a sharp jerk of the wrist. Some of the mixture should fall off.) Divide between the prepared tins, spreading out the mix gently. Bake for about 25 minutes until well risen and golden brown. Cool in the tin for 10 minutes before turning out onto a rack to cool. Spread the underside of one cake generously with jam and top with whipped cream. Lay the second sponge on top, topside up. Dust with icing sugar and serve.

Scones – Makes 12
Preheat oven to 450F. Well-floured baking sheet.

Ingredients: 4 cups self-rising flour, 4 cups all-purpose flour, 2 tsp. baking powder, 1 tsp. salt, ¼ cup butter chilled and cut into very small cubes, 1 Tbsp. lemon juice. 1⅔ cups whole milk plus extra to glaze, jam and clotted or whipped cream to serve.

Mode: Sift flour, baking powder and salt into mixing bowl and stir to mix through. Add butter and rub lightly into flour with fingertips until it resembles fine, even textured bread crumbs. Whisk lemon juice into milk and leave for about one minute to thicken slightly, then pour into flour mixture and mix quickly to make a soft, pliable dough. (The softer the mixture the lighter the scones will be, but if too sticky they will spread during baking and lose their shape.) Knead dough briefly then roll out on a lightly floured surface to a thickness of at least one inch. Using a 2" cookie cutter and dipping into flour each time, cut out 12 rounds. Place on well-floured baking sheet. Roll out any remaining dough scraps and cut more rounds. Brush the top of the scones with a little milk then put into oven and bake about 20 minutes or until risen and golden brown. Remove from oven and wrap scones in a clean dish towel to keep them warm and soft until ready to eat. Enjoy the scones with plenty of jam and cream.

Anchovy Toasts – Serves 4-6
Ingredients: 2oz. can anchovy fillets in olive oil – well drained, 6 Tbsp. soft unsalted butter, 1 Tbsp. finely chopped fresh parsley, generous squeeze of lemon juice, ground black pepper, 4-6 slices of bread.

Mode: Using mortar and pestle, crush the anchovies to make a thick paste. Add the butter, parsley and lemon juice and mix well. Season to taste with black pepper. (Alternatively, put all the ingredients into a food processor and blend into a smooth paste.) Just before serving, toast bread on both sides. Spread the anchovy butter on the hot toast, cut into fingers and serve immediately.

Recipe Index

Also from MX Publishing

MX Publishing is the world's largest specialist Sherlock Holmes publisher, with over two hundred titles and one hundred authors creating the latest in Sherlock Holmes fiction and non-fiction.

From traditional short stories and novels to travel guides and quiz books, MX Publishing cater for all Holmes fans.

The collection includes leading titles such as Benedict Cumberbatch In Transition and The Norwood Author which won the 2011 Howlett Award (Sherlock Holmes Book of the Year).

MX Publishing also has one of the largest communities of Holmes fans on Facebook with regular contributions from dozens of authors.

https://www.facebook.com/BooksSherlockHolmes

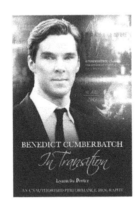

www.mxpublishing.com

"Phil Growick's, 'The Secret Journal of Dr Watson', is an adventure which takes place in the latter part of Holmes and Watson's lives. They are entrusted by HM Government (although not officially) and the King no less to undertake a rescue mission to save the Romanovs, Russia's Royal family from a grisly end at the hand of the Bolsheviks. There is a wealth of detail in the story but not so much as would detract us from the enjoyment of the story. Espionage, counter-espionage, the ace of spies himself, double-agents, double-crossers...all these flit across the pages in a realistic and exciting way. All the characters are extremely well-drawn and Mr Growick, most importantly, does not falter with a very good ear for Holmesian dialogue indeed. Highly recommended. A five-star effort."

The Baker Street Society

www.mxpublishing.com

 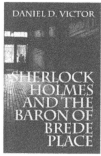 

Also from MX Publishing

The Detective and The Woman Series

The Detective and The Woman

The Detective, The Woman and The Winking Tree

The Detective, The Woman and The Silent Hive

"The book is entertaining, puzzling and a lot of fun. I believe the author has hit on the only type of long-term relationship possible for Sherlock Holmes and Irene Adler. The details of the narrative only add force to the romantic defects we expect in both of them and their growth and development are truly marvelous to watch. This is not a love story. Instead, it is a coming-of-age tale starring two of our favorite characters."

Philip K Jones

www.mxpublishing.com

 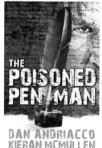 
125

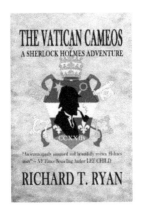

When the papal apartments are burgled in 1901, Sherlock Holmes is summoned to Rome by Pope Leo XII. After learning from the pontiff that several priceless cameos that could prove compromising to the church, and perhaps determine the future of the newly unified Italy, have been stolen, Holmes is asked to recover them. In a parallel story, Michelangelo, the toast of Rome in 1501 after the unveiling of his Pieta, is commissioned by Pope Alexander VI, the last of the Borgia pontiffs, with creating the cameos that will bedevil Holmes and the papacy four centuries later. For fans of Conan Doyle's immortal detective, the game is always afoot. However, the great detective has never encountered an adversary quite like the one with whom he crosses swords in "The Vatican Cameos.."

"An extravagantly imagined and beautifully written Holmes story"

(Lee Child, NY Times Bestselling author, Jack Reacher series)